Heal

CRYSTALS

Made Simple

—

An Hachette UK Company
www.hachette.co.uk

First published in Great Britain in 2006 as *Your Crystal Code* by Godsfield Press,
a division of Octopus Publishing Group Ltd
Carmelite House, 50 Victoria Embankment, London EC4Y 0DZ
www.octopusbooks.co.uk

This edition published in 2017 by Bounty Books, a division of Octopus Publishing Group Ltd

ISBN 978-0-7537-3273-1

A CIP catalogue record for this book is available from the British Library

Printed and bound in China

10 9 8 7 6 5 4 3 2 1

For the Bounty edition
Publisher: Lucy Pessell
Designer: Lisa Layton
Editor: Sarah Vaughan
Production Controller: Beata Kibil

Disclaimer
This book is not intended as an alternative to personal medical advice. The reader should consult a physician in all matters
relating to health and particularly in respect of any symptoms which may require diagnosis or medical attention.

Heal

CRYSTALS

Made Simple

—

CONTENTS

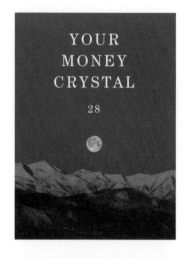
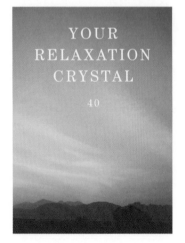

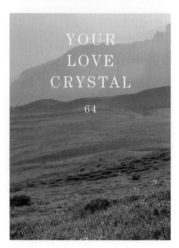

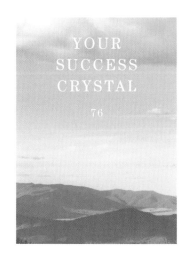

YOUR
SUCCESS
CRYSTAL
76

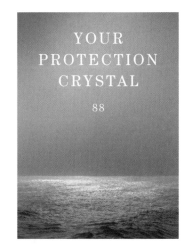

YOUR
PROTECTION
CRYSTAL
88

YOUR
MEDITATION
CRYSTAL
100

ENHANCING
YOUR LIFE
WITH CRYSTALS
112

INTRODUCTION

—

*Enter the world of crystals and be prepared to find
true magic in your life. Crystals were formed
within the Earth millions of years ago and carry
with them the wisdom of the ages.*

While all crystals absorb and emit subtle energy, each individual crystal type
has a unique vibrational 'signature'. Each crystal has a symmetrical structure
at atomic level, built with geometric precision. While it may appear tranquil
and still, at the crystal's molecular level it is a powerhouse of energy. This
'energy' is what endows a crystal with its attributes and defines the gifts it
brings.

Through the ages crystals have been worn for their beauty, as symbols of
power and divinity, or for their therapeutic and beneficial effects. They have
been used in magic and to enhance spirituality. Many people believe that
crystals are centres or channels of spiritual powers. People who worship
Nature see crystals as carrying the special blessing of the Mother Goddess.
Others believe that crystals are merely convenient tools for focusing their
mental energies. Whatever your perspective, in the following pages you will
discover your own special crystals that form a code that will help to enhance
your life in a variety of ways.

OBTAINING AND CHOOSING CRYSTALS

It has never been easier to obtain crystals – many New Age and knick-knack shops sell an array of tumble-stones (crystals that have been ground mechanically to create a smooth finish) for very little money. There are an increasing number of specialist stores solely devoted to selling lovely crystals in all shapes and sizes, as ornaments, jewellery or aids to meditation and esoteric practices.

If you have only recently become interested in crystals, allow yourself the time to collect the ones that you like, handling them, arranging them and playing with them. You may start to pick up impressions from them or feel that certain crystals have certain effects. Talk to your crystal supplier to ensure that those you buy have not been dyed or tampered with.

In each of the following chapters you will be given methods for choosing the crystal that relates to the area of life in question – love, money or relaxation, for example. All of these methods involve accessing your intuition. However, when you are choosing crystals in a shop you will not be able to perform these exercises, so you need to learn to listen to the 'call' of a crystal. Many people believe that crystals choose them. I vividly remember the evening when a heart-shaped piece of green tourmaline insisted from across the room that I buy it. It has been with me ever since helping my creativity, and is beside me as I type.

When choosing a crystal, learn to listen to your body. A crystal that is right for you may give you a sensation in the pit of your stomach, in your heart or in your head. You may feel tingling, you may even 'taste' the crystal. Possibly you may think you hear music or your eye may simply be drawn to a specific crystal. If you are not sure, relax and see what comes to mind. Hold the crystal in your palm and see what impressions you get. Or you may just know that you want a certain crystal. The ability to choose crystals may require practise, but remember you can't really get it wrong. Any crystal may be right, but some will be more right than others.

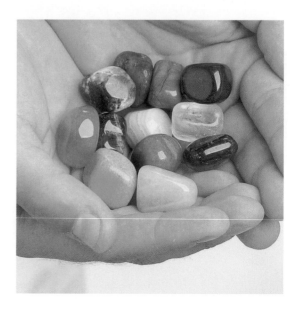

STORING CRYSTALS

It is best to store crystals away from the light wrapped in black velvet, especially if you are keeping them to use in specific exercises and rituals.

Crystals that have points may be easily damaged, while tumble-stones can be kept together in a bag. Crystals that you want to have on display or that you use frequently can be kept out, but they will need cleansing more frequently because they may pick up what is going on in the room or become polluted by electromagnetic radiation or geopathic stress. Keep crystals out of sunlight, because some stones may fade. Some exposure to sunlight may be specifically indicated in particular exercises, which is a different matter.

CLEANSING YOUR CRYSTALS

All crystals, whether tumble-stones, crystal balls, healing wands or jewellery, should be cleansed before using or wearing, because crystals pick up and absorb influences. Some people believe that some crystals never need cleansing (citrine, for instance) but it can never do any harm to cleanse a crystal, even if all that needs removing are the most superficial influences of someone else's touch. Be especially careful of crystals that have been used by another person for esoteric purposes or have been worn on the body; cleanse these thoroughly before using them.

Crystals are very delicate and should be treated with great care when cleansing. Tumble-stones are tougher, because they have been ground to a smooth and durable finish, but they still need respect. Basically, what cleanses your crystal is your intention to do so. If you are good at visualizing, place your crystal in front of you on a white cloth, and simply imagine a stream of pure water flowing through the crystal, deeply cleansing it. Do this visualization for as long as you feel necessary, and then a little longer.

If you want to do something more physical, take your crystal to a stream and hold it in the water, while affirming that all impurities are being removed. Or you may soak your crystal overnight in spring water. Never use salt water as it can damage some crystals, and be aware that some crystals, such as selenite, are water-soluble and so should never be cleansed by this method. Crystals should be allowed to dry naturally on a clean cloth; do not rub them. Crystals should be cleansed each time you use them, before being safely put away until next time.

You can also clean crystals by passing them through incense smoke; a lavender joss stick will serve this purpose admirably. Passing them through (or near) a candle flame will also do the trick. Another method suggests leaving your crystal in an earthenware bowl of unrefined brown rice overnight. The rice should be thrown away after this and never eaten.

MORE CLEANSING TIPS

- A carnelian kept in a bag with other tumble-stones will keep them all clean.
- Small crystals can be left overnight on a larger crystal cluster of clear quartz or amethyst to be cleansed.
- A bed of flower petals can be used for cleansing in a similar way to the rice bowl method.

CHARGING YOUR CRYSTALS

After choosing and cleansing your crystals you will want to charge them up with your own essence to make them truly 'yours'. You may do this simply by holding the crystal between your palms and sending energy into it, visualizing the crystal pulsating with the life force that you have imparted.

Alternatively, you may wish to perform a small ritual charge and also dedicate your crystal to divine powers. You will need a candle, a stone, a lavender joss stick and a glass with a stem (such as a wine glass) containing water. If you have a statue of a goddess or god that is meaningful to you, have this close by. You will also need your crystal.

Affirm that your ritual space is clear. Sweep it with a broom or duster as a symbol of cleansing. Imagine a protective circle surrounding you. Place the stone roughly to your north, the joss stick to the east, the candle to the south and the glass of water to the west. If you live in the southern hemisphere, reverse the positions of the candle and stone. These objects represent the four elements – earth, fire, air and water – and the directions to which they

have a time-honoured link in esoteric tradition. Place your statue by the element you prefer.

Holding your crystal in your hand face the stone and say 'I dedicate this crystal to the powers of earth, for grounding and protection'. Move sun-wise (clockwise in the northern hemisphere, anticlockwise in the south) visiting the other elements. Face the joss stick and say 'I dedicate this crystal to the powers of air, for clarity and truth'. Face the candle and say 'I dedicate this crystal to the powers of fire, for courage and energy'; finally, face the glass and say 'I dedicate this crystal to the powers of water, for healing and purity'.

Now your crystal is truly charged up. Mentally dismantle your protective circle and store your crystal with care.

SHAPES

Crystals come in many different shapes, but for the purposes of this book we are concentrating on tumble-stones, as these are cheaper, easier to handle and arrange in a balanced fashion when you form your mandala (see page 114). Crystals not available as tumble-stones should be purchased as a very small piece. However, in the case of certain special crystals it is a good idea to obtain them in other shapes – for instance, a quartz wand is invaluable for healing, and scrying is best done with a crystal in the traditional ball shape.

COLOURS

Crystals come in all the colours of the rainbow, and the colour of a crystal reveals something of its characteristics. For instance, a red crystal brings with it energy, vitality and passion, a purple one is spiritual and uplifting while a green crystal may resonate more with earthly matters, such as creativity, money and plants. However, you will find a variety of colours included in each section, to give a different nuance of meaning. Amethyst and clear quartz may have a more obvious connection to higher states, but if you are into nature mysticism, then green agate may suit you, and if you seek tantric bliss, rhodocrosite could be a better companion. It is your choice.

YOUR CRYSTAL NOTEBOOK

As you choose, care for and use your crystals, your knowledge and experience are growing. It is a good idea to record your impressions and thoughts in a notebook kept especially for your crystal code. This will be a valuable storehouse of knowledge as you become more familiar with crystals. Impressions may come to you through the crystals, or you may feel that you know something about a crystal that is not in this or any other book. You may read or hear information about crystals that is especially interesting or you may achieve an effect with a crystal that is especially memorable. Most worthy of note may be dreams that you have or experiences you go through while meditating. But most of all there is the matter of choosing each of your eight crystals, what they turn out to be and how you feel about each one. All of these things and more are worth recording in a notebook.

YOUR CRYSTAL CODE

Once you have chosen each of your crystals and used them in the exercises, you have the 'code' for balance, harmony and self-expression in your life. Each crystal embodies a certain purpose that is just for you, and channels more energy for you to use. As this takes effect, you will discover more things about yourself and move towards other realizations.

Your crystal code is not a static formula; it is dynamic and ever changing. As time goes by you may find that you wish to change one or more of your crystals; this is fine (although it is best not to change your crystals too frequently or abruptly). Apply your crystal code to all life situations and discover your path to personal fulfilment.

AN IMPORTANT NOTE

Please remember that although there are many instructions given in this book, nothing can take the place of your intuition. If you feel strongly that a crystal has a specific effect, then that is very probably correct, at least for you. You should be guided by your intuition primarily – never tell yourself you must be wrong because of something you read in a book.

For each of the following chapters a selection of 12 crystals has been suggested from which you may choose. These crystals are listed for their particular properties, each offering something different but suitable to the purpose. However, if you feel that none of the crystals listed is correct and you wish to choose something completely different, then you should follow your own inner convictions.

Another important point to keep in mind is the knowledge that crystals are very powerful, and while none are intented to cause distress, some may be hard to handle.

It is not impossible that they could cause harm to the vulnerable. An example of this concerns a young man I knew who was suffering from a brain tumour. After successful surgery he came home to the apartment he shared with his girlfriend, which was also home to several beautiful crystals. While the young man slept his highly sensitive and psychic girlfriend sat bolt upright and awake for most of the night, keeping entities from the crystals from entering through the opening in his skull. What these 'entities' may have been and whether her fears were justified I cannot be sure, but my impression certainly is that not all crystals act benign all the time. Malachite and black obsidian, for instance, have a very powerful influence that may be dangerous to sensitive, less-than-stable people who have many repressed emotions and fears. So treat crystals with respect – they have been on this planet much longer than us.

YOUR PERSONALITY CRYSTAL

—

*Perhaps the most important of your crystal choices
is your Personality Crystal. Not only is it an
expression of the real 'you' but it also represents
your potential as a person.*

The interpretation of your choice of crystal may surprise you by describing qualities you did not know you possessed, or it may seem immediately 'right'. Either way, your Personality Crystal is there to empower you and help you to become the person you are destined to be.

It is worthwhile investing in all of the listed crystals as tumble-stones, not only to make choosing easier and because they are inexpensive, but because at a later date you may want to reselect your Personality Crystal. As we go through life we change, obviously. Sometimes, however, this change may take place at a profound level. It is as if we have found another layer to our personality, or possibly as if there was another person within who has now found the light of day. This shows that we are developing as human beings.

Your Personality Crystal should facilitate this change, as you fully express that facet of your personality represented by the crystal. If and when it is appropriate, you will be able to move on. And should you wish to return to a previous crystal that is fine too. It doesn't signify a backwards step, but merely a return at a new level of experience.

CHOOSING YOUR PERSONALITY CRYSTAL

Your Personality Crystal is so special that you may not feel that you need to make any effort to 'choose'. You may feel immediately drawn to a crystal or may have loved this particular stone for some time. But if you need a little help or want to make sure, try one of the following methods.

YOU WILL NEED

Tumble-stones of the following crystals: garnet, green tourmaline, citrine, moonstone, sunstone, moss agate, blue quartz, bloodstone, ametrine, onyx, aquamarine and labradorite; or the name of the crystal written on paper. Gold candle; oils or joss sticks of frankincense or cinnamon; gold cloth.

THE CLOTH BAG METHOD

Place all the crystals or their substitutes in a cloth bag. Sit quietly with your eyes closed and relax. Be aware of your body. Let a sensation of warmth spread through you, starting as a golden glow behind your navel, gradually energizing your entire body. When you feel ready, reach into the bag and choose your stone. Visualize the glow receding back behind your navel and closing off.

THE VISUALIZATION METHOD

Place all the crystals in front of you with a gold candle behind them. Burn a joss stick of frankincense or cinnamon, or heat either of those oils in an oil burner. Light the gold candle behind the crystals.

Sit in front of the crystals and think about all that makes you 'you'. What do you like about yourself? What are you good at? How would you describe yourself? How have friends described you and what qualities have they seen in you? And what would you like to be like? Allow these thoughts to flow through your mind, then close your eyes and be still.

Now open your eyes. Which crystal draws you? Which seems to ask to be picked up? That is your Personality Crystal. If you feel undecided about two or more, take away those you feel sure are not right for you and repeat the exercise until you have eliminated all but one.

THE CRYSTAL CIRCLE METHOD

Place your crystals in a circle on a gold cloth. In the centre of the circle place a large golden candle. Around the candle place articles that are personal and precious to you – choose things that are about you as a person, not about someone or something else. For instance, a wedding or engagement ring is about your relationship, your purse is about money, but a small teddy bear you had as a child, your diary or any article you acquired simply because you loved it are truer expressions of yourself.

Light the candle and burn incense as for the visualization method. Relax and become steady and calm. Start to focus on the crystals. Which one do you feel should join your special possessions around the candle? Perhaps the candlelight glints on one crystal more brightly than on the others. Maybe you feel more drawn to one crystal.

THE VISUALIZATION METHOD TWO

Lay the crystals out and burn candle and incense as for the visualization method. Let yourself be calm and peaceful. Cast your mind back to a time when you felt particularly happy, complete, fulfilled and recognized (or just one or two of those descriptions). Which crystal seems the best expression of that time? It may seem to shine brighter as you visualize.

Sometimes you may find that several crystals seem to respond to your happy thoughts. If so, narrow down your choice with successive attempts until you are left with the one that responds most strongly. This crystal is your best choice.

INTERPRETING YOUR PERSONALITY CRYSTAL

BLOODSTONE

Intense and passionate, you love and hate with equal strength. You find it hard to forgive and forget, and will often make sure you get your own back. However, for a true friend you are prepared to 'walk through the Valley of Death'. Your courage and determination are unbeatable and you are generous with your help and sympathy, although you prefer to help those who also help themselves. To you, knowledge is power and you like to get to the bottom of things.

In relationships, once you give your heart it is for good, and you can be jealous as well as deeply empathic. It is important for you to have periods alone in order to regenerate yourself and feel 're-born'.

You are often best at behind-the-scenes work, using your DEDUCTIVE abilities, but you can also be DRAMATIC and ARTISTIC.

CITRINE

You are a dynamic, lively person with a smile on your face. Your mind is always active; you have a hunger for knowledge, but require more than just facts. It is important for you to have your powers of reason stimulated and to be able to come to your own conclusions. You love to communicate; whether this is about deep matters or some entertaining gossip, you can be very witty.

In relationships mental rapport is essential to you, along with shared cultural interests. A great flirt, you are not too eager to commit yourself and often change your mind. Be careful not to be too 'in the head' – gut feelings and emotions are just as important as ideas.

Professions such as PUBLISHING and the MEDIA may appeal and your INGENUITY can take you far in life.

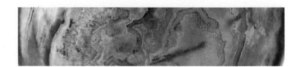

ONYX

Practical and restrained, you value common sense and security, and like to feel you are progressing steadily in life. It is important to you to be in control of as many things as possible – like the Boy Scouts, your motto is 'Be prepared'. You can be pessimistic and may erect barriers in life by trying to be one step ahead.

In relationships you tend to be reserved; you do not like to give too much away about your feelings and sometimes you are not sure what they are. Once you decide someone is suitable for you, however, you support that person in all ways and you are a committed family member.

You work best where your PLANNING and CONSTRUCTING abilities are utilized; you are capable of PATIENCE in achieving long-term goals.

GARNET

You are an energetic and enterprising person, sometimes jumping in where angels fear to tread. Patience is not your virtue, and you often lose interest in things that take too long. A person of initiative and ideas, you prefer to sow rather than to stay around and reap. You have great courage and leadership qualities and you take a positive attitude to life, although when things do not go your way you can become angry and moody.

Prepared to stick up for yourself and your friends where necessary, you can be bossy and aggressive, but also generous, responsible and good at organizing. Don't worry if some say you are self-important as long as you keep things in proportion and remain effective.

You work best where your DRIVE and MANAGERIAL talents can have full scope and where you can take the INITIATIVE.

GREEN TOURMALINE

You are patient and persevering. You love stability and security and do your best to create this around you. Practical things such as money and creature comforts are important. You take a realistic, pragmatic approach to life, preferring to believe the evidence of your senses, although you are aware of ambience and love peace.

Affectionate, kind and dependable, you can be very stubborn sometimes and resistant to anything new. What's yours is yours and you can be possessive but you will offer help to those you love.

You are probably good at gardening, having an affinity with growing things and cooking may also appeal to you since you are drawn to all forms of pleasure and life's bounty.

You love CREATIVE pursuits and are at your best in any profession that offers you STABILITY, COMFORT, good pay and an outlet for your artistic talents.

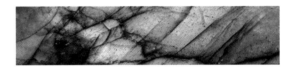

LABRADORITE

Imaginative and mystical, sometimes it seems you are closer to the world of the spirit than to this world. You are a deeply sympathetic and empathic individual, feeling the ills of others as if they were your own. You need to protect yourself from too many demands, since you find it hard to say 'no'. Change is your middle name, since you see so many sides to everything that it is impossible to find one way of being, one point of view that fits everything.

Your emotions are very strong and you tend to go through life being in love with a person or thing. Artistic and creative, you often find it hard to stick at one thing, being easily distracted. You are very idealistic and sensitive and you need time on your own to help you recharge your batteries. Follow your dreams and keep your feet on the ground.

You prefer to be INDEPENDENT in your work, but you need to know that it is MEANINGFUL and/or CREATIVE.

MOONSTONE

Your emotions and instincts are very strong, making you extremely protective of yourself and those whom you love. Home and family are central to your existence and you are a nurturing, supportive person. However, you can also be touchy and moody – if someone hurts you this may never be forgotten, for your memory is excellent.

Your dreams are very important to you and you are very intuitive, but you are also practical, managing money wisely and able to sense whom you can trust. Closeness and empathy are vital and you need to feel loved and understood. It is very hard for you to let go of the past and anything that represents it, so you can be an indiscriminate hoarder.

You function best when your sympathetic, CARING nature is valued, where your TENACITY is respected and your PRIVACY is not invaded.

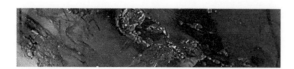

MOSS AGATE

Refined and discriminating, you have the instincts of an epicure. No detail passes you by and you are an excellent organizer. Able to get to the root of most things, you are a 'fixer', practical, tidy and thorough. Being useful is important to you and you are happiest when busy and needed by others.

You can be modest and self-effacing, although if you are taken for granted this makes you unhappy. You are your own worst critic and therefore all the more sensitive to criticism from others, although you are very aware of the shortcomings of other people. Sometimes you favour a hands-on approach and you can achieve wonderful things in garden, kitchen and office as long as you try to relax.

Your HIGH STANDARDS, EFFICIENCY and passion for EXCELLENCE need to find expression in your work.

AMETRINE

You are adventurous and far-seeing, often so preoccupied with possibilities and philosophies that you may not see what is under your nose. Freedom is very important to you, and you probably like to travel, either literally or mentally. You seek always to expand your experience and education, learning about foreign cultures and religions, bringing what they have to offer into your own life and using it enthusiastically.

Usually optimistic and generous, you take a positive attitude to life and encourage others to do the same. Sometimes you can be careless because your mind is far away, and you can be inconsiderate, reckless and tactless – but you are nonetheless warm-hearted.

You function best where your ENERGY and ENTHUSIASM can have full rein and where you can ENCOURAGE others to appreciate life as you do!

AQUAMARINE

Being an individual is the most important thing to you, and you tend to live your life to the beat of a 'different drum'. Although you like to have a wide circle of friends, you are not eager to let anyone too close because this could cramp your style. Highly original, inventive and even rebellious at times, you pursue your own ideals, for these are the stuff of life to you.

You may change your mind a hundred times but no one will change it for you, and sometimes you can be eccentric, stubborn and awkward. Although you may be very intellectual, you hate being cooped up at a desk. You seek the truth and are very concerned with the welfare of humans, animals and the planet itself, so you may be involved with charitable concerns.

You need to be where you can be FREE and independent and where there is scope for your RESOURCEFULNESS and UNIQUE perspective.

SUNSTONE

Your main drive in life is to shine as brightly as you can wherever you are, whatever you are doing. Proud and dignified, you are usually well respected for your reliability, generosity and the strength of your personality. Your faith in life is considerable and your attitude is noble to the point that you often miss small details.

Because you are very idealistic and honest, you can be very hurt when others let you down. Although you are magnanimous, joyful and loving, you can also be a little bossy and conceited on occasion, and sometimes you show off.

You function best where there is plenty of scope for your sense of drama; you like to bask in the LIMELIGHT and use your AUTHORITY, and can be good at MANAGING large-scale projects.

BLUE QUARTZ

Beautiful surroundings and a peaceful atmosphere are as necessary to you as the air you breathe and you do your best to please everyone. In fact, it is often hard for you to make up your mind as you try to fit in with both sides. However, while you may appear pliable and biddable, you have a laser-sharp brain and anyone who tries to take advantage of you sooner or later finds themselves gently, firmly and cleverly put in their place!

Tactful and gracious, you probably have wonderful manners and dress sense. Sometimes, however, you can be lazy and procrastinating, a quiet life being the most important thing on your agenda along with regular retail therapy. You cannot function where there is ugliness and discord.

You should seek a place where your TALENT for DIPLOMACY and your eye for what is lovely are APPRECIATED.

PERSONALITY PLUS VISUALIZATION

Your crystal can help you shine in life by focusing your own special talents and energies. Because your Personality Crystal is a concentration of your own energies, it can serve to intensify your best and strongest characteristics. Try this simple visualization when you have to speak in public or on the first day of a new job. Or do it whenever you need to feel special and empowered.

1 Lie down comfortably in a dimly lit room. Burn oils/incense of frankincense or cinnamon to help create the right atmosphere. Relax and place your crystal on your navel. Imagine that the crystal is starting to glow brighter and brighter. Feel the radiance within your body – beautiful, warming, exciting. Enjoy the feeling.

2 Now imagine an answering glow from behind your navel combining with that of the crystal so that you are suffused with brilliance. Visualize the light growing and extending, encircling you in an egg shape. When you are ready, visualize yourself in the coming situation, but doing it wonderfully, feeling truly uplifted and pleased with yourself. Hold this visualization as long as you can.

3 When you are ready, come back to ordinary awareness. Pat your body to make sure you are properly grounded and make any necessary notes in your journal. Be sure to take the crystal with you when you face the challenge.

ATTRACTING FRIENDS RITUAL

What do you want from friendship? Maybe it is support, laughter, someone to share your interests and to accompany you on outings. Do all these things have to come from one person or would several people be fine?

1 Spread out your pot-pourri on your tray or plate and place your Personality Crystal in the centre. Holding your stones, allow yourself to reflect on what you want from a friendship. Try not to be too picky, as no one is perfect. Reflect on what you bring to friendship – the help and advice you might give, for instance. Allow yourself to feel valuable.

2 When you are ready, place each of the stones in turn on the edge of the tray, naming the quality that each represents if you like, or simply visualize each one as a desirable companion. Imagine clearly that there are people out there just waiting to get to know you.

3 Each morning when you get up, move the stones a little closer to your crystal until they are touching. Meanwhile, follow up on every invite you get, however unsuitable it may seem at first. Repeat this exercise if you need to, but initially leave the stones touching your crystal for at least a month. Note anything significant in your journal.

YOU WILL NEED

Pink pot-pourri; a tray, large plate or box lid on which to spread it; some small stones to represent friends or the qualities you look for in a friend.

WEARING YOUR CRYSTAL

More than any of your other crystals you will want to wear your Personality Crystal to enhance your special qualities and to feel powerful.

HOW TO WEAR YOUR CRYSTAL

Your crystal has a slightly different effect according to which part of the body it is adorning.

NECKLACE

This stimulates your ability to express yourself verbally, which is excellent for any form of speaking, negotiating, communicating or talking at parties.

PENDANT

Worn near your heart, it stimulates your sympathetic responses to people you meet, enabling you to make a strong impression.

EARRINGS

Your ears are attuned to anything that can enhance your feeling of 'specialness' such as compliments and heightened understanding.

NOSE STUD

Gives you an instinct for being in the right place at the right time.

NAVEL STUD

Enhances your personal power, although navel piercings are not popular with acupuncturists as the navel is on an important meridian and interfering with it could cause depression, so be aware.

FINGER RING

Your creativity and effectiveness will be increased by wearing your crystal on your hand: index finger – leadership; second finger – practical and enduring achievement; third finger – artistic endeavour; little finger – writing and communication; thumb – independence. The meanings are more receptive than active in your least dominant hand; in a right-handed person the third finger of the left hand relates more to appreciating the beautiful than actually creating it.

BRACELET

Increases your openness to opportunities and your ability to seize them.

ANKLET

Gives you the confidence to explore and to draw from your experiences all that can help you grow and develop.

TOE RING

Takes you on wonderful adventures to discover many things about yourself.

SELF-DEVELOPMENT VISUALIZATION

Taking the time to reflect on your development with your Personality Crystal can be deeply rewarding.

1 Lie down where you won't be disturbed and relax deeply. Holding your crystal in one of your palms, let your mind drift. Imagine walking down a narrow country road. Look around and notice the trees and fields, the green of the plants, the blue of the sky. Listen to the sounds, perhaps of lowing cattle or the rustling of the breeze. Be aware of the sun on your skin, the breeze in your hair and all the scents of the country, the richness of the earth, the sweetness of new-mown grass. Feel your feet making solid contact with the ground – really be there. This should feel as real as possible.

2 You now come to a crossroads. One path leads up a hill – the road bends and twists so you cannot see along it but you can spot in the distance that it eventually leads high up a steep and rocky slope. Another path leads deep into the darkness of a forest and another down to a lake. Which one should you take?

4 The spirit of your crystal will now lead you down one of the paths. Be assured that you are safe with your crystal spirit. All that you see now is personal to you. Explore but do not jump to conclusions.

3 Now be aware that a spirit is materializing from your crystal and holding your hand. Take the trouble to visualize your crystal spirit. Commune if you wish.

5 When you are ready, thank the crystal spirit, say goodbye and come back to everyday awareness, pat your body and drink some water to ground yourself. Write down all you remember in your journal. What did your experience convey about your development?

YOUR
MONEY
CRYSTAL

—

*Depending on your personality and
circumstances, you will have your own
specific requirements with regard to money.
Some people are very good at managing or
acquiring money; others are not.*

Circumstances vary from person to person. You may need money urgently for some particular project or purpose or you may have received a legacy and need to spend and invest wisely. Psychological issues around money may be more important for you; for instance, do you have a 'poverty consciousness' where you behave as if you are poor, even when you are comfortably off? Or does money just run through your fingers? Maybe you are a retail junkie or find it hard to budget. Possibly you are drawn to gambling, or you simply keep losing your purse. Whatever the issues and the situation, your choice of Money Crystal can help you become balanced and prosperous.

It is best to have a sample of each of the crystals as tumble-stones, but if this is not possible then use pictures of the particular crystals. You may find the final method of selection difficult to perform if you only use paper representations.

CHOOSING YOUR MONEY CRYSTAL

Before selecting your crystal it is important to relax and to reflect on your needs and situation in life. This allows you to focus your consciousness on the choice, although sometimes the crystal chosen has a message of its own that helps you to understand yourself better. This is part of the crystal gift.

YOU WILL NEED

Tumble-stones of the following crystals: jade, tiger's eye, aventurine, bloodstone, calcite, chrysoprase, peridot, sapphire, green tourmaline, gold topaz, green quartz and spinel. Green candle; gold candle; oil or joss sticks of patchouli; green cloth; organic brown rice; earthenware bowl.

THE CLOTH BAG METHOD

Place the crystals or paper representations of them into a cloth bag. Think clearly about your finances and what you would most like help with. When you are ready reach into the bag and draw out a crystal.

THE CANDLE METHOD

Lay the tumble-stones or pictures out before you on a green cloth (green is traditionally associated with money). Light a green candle behind the crystals and place your cheque book, credit card and purse or wallet in front of them. Place any other article or document that is especially important to your finances there as well.

Sit in front of your stones and close your eyes. Ask to be shown the stone that will be most helpful to you in your financial situation. When you are ready, open your eyes. You should now have a sense of which crystal to choose – probably the one on which your eyes alighted first or your choice may be indicated by shadows thrown by the candle.

THE RICE BOWL METHOD

You will need the actual tumble-stone versions of your crystals for this method and some organic brown rice in an earthenware bowl (because of its nourishing qualities, rice is traditionally linked to wealth). Lay out your crystals before you on a green cloth with the green and gold candles. Light the candles and the patchouli incense/oil and sit, relaxed, in front of the crystals.

Place your right hand (or left, if left-handed) into the bowl of rice and indulge yourself with a fantasy of wealth. Now pick up the crystals in turn while you imagine this abundance. What do you feel with each crystal? Which enhances your fantasy the best? You may have to do this exercise several times, eliminating crystals each time until you arrive at your final choice. You will be left with your money crystal.

THE CRYSTAL CIRCLE METHOD

Try this if you feel you have a special money problem that you wish to overcome, such as gambling. Do it on a green cloth or carpet if possible. Burn oil or a joss stick of patchouli and place your crystals or their substitutes in a wide circle on the cloth.

Sit in the centre of the circle and think about your problem. Visualize yourself in the situation that you find difficult to control; for instance, when you are out shopping. In this situation you need a guardian at your elbow to restrain you with good advice. Imagine this gentle, wise and firm guardian is arising out of one of the crystals – which one is it?

THE VISUALIZATION METHOD

If you able to visualize and have an emotional issue concerning money, this may be a good method for you. Lay your crystals out as described in the Candle Method, without bothering with the documents and credit cards. Sit in front of the crystals or their representations and imagine yourself in the relevant challenging situation, such as speaking to your bank manager or negotiating a settlement with your ex. Now which of the crystals do you most want to hold in your hand?

INTERPRETING YOUR MONEY CRYSTAL

JADE

This stone helps you to think positively about money, to value what you possess and enables you to use it wisely. It stimulates your creativity with regard to money-making enterprises and has the ability to attract money. However, jade is a spiritual stone and will enable you to have a balanced attitude to your finances, realizing that the most important riches are not to be found in any bank account.

If you have chosen jade, then it may be that you need to stop worrying about money. This stone will help you to expel negative thoughts and to realize that management of money is essentially a simple matter. Wearing jade jewellery attracts money and helps you receive it gracefully.

Jade will help you to feel SELF-SUFFICIENT and INDEPENDENT, AWARE of the resources that you possess and able to utilize them.

TIGER'S EYE

This very protective stone was once worn as a protection against curses and all forms of danger. Tiger's eye is a fine stone to have if your finances are under any sort of threat, especially from theft or swindling. This stone is grounding and yet enlightening – it can enable you to see clearly 'with the eye of the tiger'. Because of this it can help you to recognize what your true needs are and to distinguish between your needs and those of other people.

If you have chosen tiger's eye then possibly you feel your money is under threat. Or maybe you feel vulnerable because you have little trust in your ability to make money. Hold tiger's eye in sunlight and look within it to open your mind to inspiration.

Tiger's eye will give you FAITH in your talents and the STRENGTH to face and OVERCOME your weaknesses.

AVENTURINE

Aventurine attracts prosperity – it helps to turn situations that are apparently disadvantageous into opportunities for gain. It can help you to spot profitable alternatives such as niches in the market if you are in business, or companies that are about to 'take off' if you are investing. Aventurine is the gambler's stone, bringing good luck but also fostering that state of calm that preserves a 'poker face'. It brings the peaceful poise that encourages intuition.

If you have chosen aventurine then maybe you need a little more courage, more 'devil-may-care' in your attitude to money, not in order to be foolish, but gambling what you can well afford to lose in order to attract opportunity. Possibly you have been too uptight about money or maybe you just need a boost of faith in yourself.

SPECULATE to ACCUMULATE. Carry aventurine whenever you take a CHANCE.

BLOODSTONE

This stone of strength can help you to adjust to challenging circumstances. If you have chosen bloodstone then you may need to stop worrying about your financial future and concentrate on the here and now, since that is all you can have control over.

If your money situation is satisfactory, bloodstone protects your interests but also enables you to judge whom to trust and whom to avoid. If you are considering helping someone financially by lending or investing, bloodstone will help you decide whether they deserve it or can be relied on. A bloodstone kept in a till or cash register is said to draw more money to it.

With the support of this stone a difficult SITUATION can be TRANSFORMED gradually and with hard work into one of stability and secure PROSPERITY.

GREEN CALCITE

Green calcite will help you to let go of old mental patterns concerning money, such as 'poverty consciousness', beliefs such as 'I never win anything' or feelings of not deserving to be rich. It can help you to grow conceptually, so you can clearly picture wealth, which is the first step towards gaining it.

If you have chosen calcite then perhaps you need to move away from your outworn beliefs about money and start picturing yourself as rich. Do not always buy the cheapest – send your subconscious messages of abundance by having the best once in a while. Calcite may double the effectiveness of an enterprise if placed in a significant spot, such as with contracts.

Calcite is especially good at DRAWING money into the HOME, so it should have pride of place in the 'MONEY CORNER' or on the hearth next to a green candle.

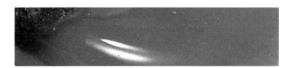

CHRYSOPRASE

This stone helps you to feel part of a beautiful, inter-connected Universe. It promotes good faith in business interests and encourages a calm state of mind that brings openness to opportunity. It helps you to rise above compulsive and impulsive spending and to direct efforts and finances in positive directions.

If you have chosen chrysoprase you may need to leave behind an extravagance that brings you no enduring pleasure. It can stop you being greedy for that next retail 'fix' and helps you to use money in accordance with your ideals. It will help you to see where you went wrong in the past and help you correct mistakes. Carry chrysoprase with you to attract money, especially if your income depends on 'the gift of the gab'.

Chrysoprase brings a sense of relaxation and TRUST in LIFE that invites LUCK.

PERIDOT

If you have bad habits with regard to money, peridot can help you leave these behind. If you tend to be miserly, this stone can help you see that this is counterproductive, and to set up a healthy flow of financial energy in your life. It can also banish envy, both your own and others, towards you, and protect you from jealous attack.

If you have chosen peridot then you may need to face certain attitudes that you have towards money and to recognize that these may not be healthy. This stone will stop you blaming others and help you to take full responsibility for your attitudes and actions. If you have business cards, it is a good idea to store them under a piece of peridot to infuse them with luck.

Peridot will help you form a clear IDEA of what CHANGES are NECESSARY and to bring them about.

SAPPHIRE

This stone attracts gifts in the form of wealth and possessions as well as more abstract gifts in the form of advice and information. It helps you to focus on the matter in hand and to feel cheerful and upbeat, believing that life is joyful.

If you have chosen sapphire it may be that you need a generous handout to help you out of a hole. Or possibly you need an influx of energy, creativity and positive thought, which will attract money. Either way, the stone will help in attracting these things but also in maintaining serenity. It repels fraud and so is an effective stone to have if you are involved in any litigation involving money – as long as you are in the right.

Sapphire was considered especially MAGICAL by the ancients, with the power to STRENGTHEN any ENTERPRISE.

GREEN TOURMALINE

This calming and grounding stone enables you to appreciate the value of money, to keep a balanced attitude and to be practical. It attracts gifts, but also encourages you to value what you already have, without continually hankering after extras.

If you have chosen green tourmaline you may need some patience and steadiness in your financial affairs. It may also indicate that you need to use your creativity to attract wealth. If you have been panicking over financial issues the gentle influence of this stone will enable you to get things in perspective. Place it in a money box to attract coins and wear it to help creativity.

Green tourmaline is especially good for giving you the CONFIDENCE and SERENITY to deal with your BOSS if he or she is something of a parent figure.

GOLD TOPAZ

A stimulating but soothing stone, topaz will help you to sort out short- and long-term financial goals and work towards them. If you have chosen topaz you may need to be put on track, or to make plans for your future. Or possibly you are financially well organized but need a little inspiration to make your money work harder for you.

It is a great stone to help in finding solutions to problems and will help you to throw light on details without losing the plot. In ancient times it was believed this stone could confer invisibility. Wear it to deflect the attention of anyone who is out to get your money, from thieves to traffic wardens.

Topaz makes you FEEL RICH, but also able to ENJOY all the things in life that MONEY CAN'T BUY.

GREEN QUARTZ

This stone will help you deal with waste, enabling you to husband your resources and get the most for least. If you have chosen green quartz you may feel that you are haemorrhaging money and need help to stem the flow. If money is not a problem, green quartz can stimulate your charitable instincts, enabling you to target your generosity wisely.

It stimulates the memory, enabling you to recall past mistakes so you do not repeat them, and to see how you created success, in order to build on it. Wear green quartz in order to attract the 'easy life'.

Green quartz has a wide range of INFLUENCE and will HEAL financial ILLS and imbalances of all descriptions.

SPINEL

Spinel offers hope and encouragement even when things are at their most dire. If you have chosen spinel you may have been deluged by financial misfortune. This stone will enable you to laugh at your situation and turn the tide in your favour. On the other hand, if things are going well, spinel reminds you to give thanks where it is due and to retain humility.

It stimulates compassion so, if someone is being mean towards you, wear or display green spinel where they can see it. If you feel that you can't be bothered to sort out a financial situation and that it is all too much, place spinel beside you on your desk for an influx of energy.

Traditionally, spinel attracts wealth, but will also give you the physical STRENGTH to EARN money and to FIGHT for what is yours – perhaps a legacy.

ATTRACTING ABUNDANCE VISUALIZATION

You can have an abundance of life's goodies – believe this is so and what you want will flow towards you. This is no great mystery, for if you change your consciousness and your beliefs, without realizing it you will begin to behave slightly differently. Gradually, you will attract wealth.

1 Lay out your scarf and place your bowl in the west, candle in the south, joss stick in the east and wheat/nuts in the north. If you live in the southern hemisphere, change the north/south placements. Light your candle and joss stick and feel peaceful.

2 Face your candle, sitting comfortably with your crystal in your palm. Now imagine good news about jobs or payments flowing from the direction of your joss stick into your crystal, energy and opportunity from your candle, support from helpful people from your bowl and possessions and cash from your wheat/nuts. Feel the richness flow into you from the crystal.

3 Do this visualization for as long as is comfortable – a few minutes will do. You can repeat it as often as you like.
One of the good things about this exercise is that you feel rich immediately!

YOU WILL NEED

A golden bowl, a cinnamon, patchouli or orange joss stick, some ears of wheat and a golden candle symbolizing the four traditional elements of water, air, earth and fire respectively; a large golden scarf to sit on. (If you cannot obtain ears of wheat substitute almonds, pine nuts, acorns or rice in an earthenware dish.)

HEALTHY ATTITUDE TO MONEY MEDITATION

It is all too easy to fear poverty and this can paralyze wise investment of all kinds. The symbolism behind this little meditation will help you to relax and have faith in life's bounty.

1 Find a quiet place where you can unwind and won't be disturbed. Play music if you like. Doing this meditation in sunshine would be beneficial. If this is not possible, light a gold candle to set the mood while you settle. Place your crystal on your lap.

2 Imagine yourself sitting beside a golden stream, with your back propped up against a soft, mossy bank. Around you the grass is lush and green, and the sun is shining warm upon you. You can hear the singing of birds and the peaceful gurgle of the flowing water. In the air there is the scent of orange blossom, and in your hand you hold the smooth stem of a large goblet, made of your crystal.

3 Watch the rippling water as it glistens in the sunlight. It is clear and fresh, flowing ceaselessly onwards, always moving, always plentiful. Look at it for a while, musing. Lean down and fill your goblet with the water – see how it sparkles! Empty and refill the goblet as many times as you wish; take a drink, if you like. Or you can simply relax, holding the goblet on your lap, savouring the peace. Do this for as long as you like.

4 When you are ready, come back to everyday awareness and record in your notebook any thoughts that occur to you.

A feeling of abundance starts in the mind.

WISE SPENDING RITUAL

Spending wisely means spending money for the right reasons (not just to cheer yourself up), making the right choices and keeping to a reasonable budget. This means remaining in touch with your true wishes. Your crystal can keep you connected to these.

1 You can do this little ritual before going shopping (this includes from catalogues or on the Internet) or at any time you feel the need. Place your bracelet, tumble-stone and original crystal in front of you.

2 Gaze deeply at your crystal and close your eyes. Imagine the spirit of the crystal rising – it may take any form but brings with it a sense of wisdom, balance and practicality. Feel this spirit flowing all over you. Imagine the colour of your crystal emanating from it and surrounding you, forming a protective shield. This is your protection against unwise spending and is also a magnet for correct purchases. Hold this image for as long as feels comfortable and listen for any words or impressions that may come from the spirit.

3 When you are ready, thank the spirit and ask it to return to the crystal. Place the bracelet on your wrist, saying three times 'Guard me from unwise spending, draw to me what I need'. Place the tumble-stone in your purse or wallet – and go shopping!

YOU WILL NEED

Your crystal in a bracelet in any form, either as a string of tumble-stones or polished and set in metal. It is also a good idea to have a small tumble-stone of your crystal to place in your purse or wallet.

MONEY MANAGEMENT EXERCISE

If you find it hard to manage money, place your crystal with your accounts or in the place where you keep bills, statements, mortgage information, cheque book and credit cards. Affirm that you are in control of your finances, aided by your crystal.

1 Do this little exercise to affirm to your subconscious mind that your money is well-managed and all your 'pots' are full. Place the sesame seeds in a bowl with your crystal, and leave them overnight to absorb the crystal essence. Work out your budget – don't be pedantic about this but make sure you do not leave out anything important.

2 Allot one jar for each category – food, clothes, mortgage, fun, holidays and so on. Spoon sesame seeds into each pot, roughly in proportion to how you have budgeted – if you spend twice as much on your mortgage as you do on food, the 'mortgage' jar should have double the sesame seeds compared with the 'food' jar. Add food colours and shake.

3 Display your jars near the spot where you deal with your accounts. Refresh the jars with new seeds every few months. You can vary this exercise in any way you want, using sweets, nuts or spices and eating the contents. As long as you refresh and renew and keep the proportions correct, that's fine. Whenever you look at your jars you will have a sense of control and plenitude.

YOU WILL NEED

Sesame seeds, several different food colours and a selection of small, transparent pots that look attractive – spice jars are ideal.

YOUR
RELAXATION
CRYSTAL

—

Your Relaxation Crystal will help you to unwind
in the way best suited to you. However, it is asking
a lot of your crystal to expect it to teach you how to
relax if you are used to being uptight!

In order to be able to tune in to your Relaxation Crystal enough to choose the one that is right for you, it may be necessary to learn the basics of relaxation. This will stand you in good stead for many of the exercises in this book and will be a great help when you meditate.

All manner of serious physical ailments, such as stroke and heart disease, are linked to stress. Stress depresses the immune system and can result in many things, from recurrent infections to painful migraines.

Relaxation, as we are coming to understand, is vital to our health. It is also vital to the expansion of consciousness. Tension is the one major barrier that comes between you and your intuition, your inner wisdom and your capacity for true joy. Learning to relax in body and mind is a skill that most of us in the West need to learn.

Let us begin.

PRACTISING YOUR RELAXATION TECHNIQUE

Your unconscious mind is like a child, and, child-like, it responds best to routine. Once your unconscious has learned the principles of relaxation it will become automatic. Channels are then opened both for creative playfulness and also for the transmission of inspiration.

Begin your relaxation practice by deciding on a time of day when you are able to relax for ten minutes. This needs to be done every day! If you miss one day out of seven, this is not the end of the world, but if you do this right at the beginning it will take longer to establish your pattern. Relaxing once a week for an hour is certainly no substitute, although it may be better than nothing; most likely you will find that it is not possible and will either fall asleep or find yourself mulling over your problems.

1 If you are an early bird, the morning may be best to begin. Get ready for the day ten minutes earlier and settle for your relaxation. Children and pets should be kept out. Turn your phone onto silent mode. As you become more skilled you may fall asleep, in which case you need to adopt a more alert position, sitting up in a chair or cross-legged on the floor. For the moment, lie on your bed, because that says 'relax!' to your unconscious. Lavender oil heated in a burner or placed on your temples can help, and/or play soft music. A relaxing tea such as camomile can also help if you tend to be anxious.

2 Bring your consciousness into your body and be very aware of your comfort. Count yourself in by saying 'One, relax, two, relax, three, relax.' Focus on your feet, feeling all the muscles in them, tensing them slightly and then relaxing. This process of tensing makes you aware of your muscles and helps you to relax them. Now move on up your legs, tensing and relaxing, then focus on your pelvis, buttocks, internal muscles, abdomen, back, chest and shoulders – pay special attention to this prime tension site. Travel all the way down your arms, into your fingers, clenching your fists and relaxing. Finally, the myriad muscles in your neck, jaw, face and scalp need the screw-up-and-relax routine.

3 Once you are relaxed visualize yourself somewhere very pleasant. Concentrate on what you see, hear, smell and touch – do not be distracted into imagining scenarios, however pleasant or into memories. If you begin to do this, draw back into your body and do a quick relaxation check before taking yourself back to your beautiful place. At the end of your relaxation, count yourself back up by saying 'Three, two, one, awaken'. Consciously ground yourself by patting your body or eating and drinking something.

CHOOSING YOUR RELAXATION CRYSTAL

When you are reasonably good at relaxing you can choose your crystal. Naturally you will be impatient, but try to allow two weeks of regular relaxation, if you can. If you cannot wait, it is not the end of the world, for none of the crystals will hinder you. However, you may want to choose again at a later date.

RELAXATION METHOD ONE

Set out all the crystals or representations in the form of pictures or their names written on slips of paper close to you when you are relaxing. Go into your relaxation routine as outlined on the previous page and concentrate totally on your body. Then go to your pleasant place. At this point you may get a vivid sense of which crystal to choose. If so, go with this choice.

RELAXATION METHOD TWO

Set out all the crystals or representations in the form of pictures or their names written on slips of paper close to you when you are relaxing as in the above method. Go into your relaxation routine as outlined on the previous page and concentrate totally on your body. Then go to your pleasant place. Continue with your relaxation in the same way as normal and come back to everyday awakening when you are ready. When you come out of your relaxation and before grounding yourself, ask yourself which crystal 'feels right'. A crystal may occur to you at this point and this is your Relaxation Crystal.

Your crystal will help you relax in any way you wish, whether this is by going more deeply into states of meditation or by more active methods such as art, creativity, play or sport.

YOU WILL NEED

Crystals to choose from include rose quartz, sugilite, lepidolite, aquamarine, gold calcite, pink chalcedony, aragonite, blue tourmaline, smithsonite, rhodochrosite, prehnite and red jasper.

INTERPRETING YOUR RELAXATION CRYSTAL

AQUAMARINE

This wonderful stone is for people who are over-sensitive; it calms their fears, helping them to get things into perspective and to use, in a positive manner, the information their almost psychic senses acquire. If you have chosen this stone, you may need its soothing influence, especially to bring something troublesome to a satisfactory end, so that you can relax and get on with life.

If you feel burdened by responsibility, aquamarine will help you to cope and feel worthwhile. On a physical note, if your favourite form of recreation is a watersport such as boating, swimming or diving, then traditionally this is the perfect stone to wear, both to keep you safe and to attune you to the relaxing blessings of water.

Aquamarine can also get you out of a boring RUT by WIDENING your PERSPECTIVE.

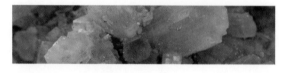

ARAGONITE

If you have chosen this crystal then the chances are that physical relaxation is of paramount importance to you and you want to feel comfortable in your body. Possibly you are a sensuous person and make judgements on the basis of practicality, or it may also be that your intuition expresses itself physically, as in 'gut feelings' and the like. At the other extreme, if you have become 'spaced out', aragonite will bring you firmly and reassuringly back to the here and now.

Aragonite warms the body and helps with conditions such as restless legs. If you push yourself too hard at work, aragonite reminds you to ease up and nurture yourself; it is a great friend if cooking is your hobby.

It teaches you that your BODY is the TEMPLE of your SOUL and that respect for its needs is essential to all occupations and enjoyment.

GOLD CALCITE

Gold calcite drives away the cobwebs and brings a breath of fresh air into your life. If you have become a bit of a couch potato you may choose gold calcite to get you moving, and so experience the relaxing benefits of exercise, possibly in the open air. Gold calcite will also attract you if you are already active, but want to develop this.

It clears the mind, enabling you to make intelligent choices about your leisure. It is excellent for sharpening the brain if you like crosswords and puzzles. It is hard to feel despondent with this stone close by. Gold calcite inspires a sense of possibilities and is a great motivator.

It is a great stone to keep you CALM and FOCUSED when STUDYING and so will help you choose the correct evening class and keep at it.

PINK CHALCEDONY

If you enjoy recreation with a group of friends, chalcedony will help retain harmony and cooperation. This is a stone for happiness and goodwill. If you have been troubled by nightmares, pink chalcedony will take you to a deeper level of relaxation, where you are in contact only with peaceful realms and so experience regenerating sleep.

Pink chalcedony will keep you aware of the magic in the world and help you to enjoy fantasy and stories. It is a great companion if you enjoy novels but may also inspire you to entertain others. Reading aloud is helped by pink chalcedony. This stone gently encourages you to try new things, having faith in the bounty of the world to bring you enjoyment.

One of its gifts is to STOP you worrying about your health and to EASE psychosomatic SYMPTOMS.

RED JASPER

Red jasper gives a boost to your get-up-and-go. It is a great stone to choose if you love sports because it will give you determination and staying power, and that competitive edge. However, this is very much

an aid to relaxation and recreation, for it takes you out of your ordinary routine so that you can forget about stresses and cares while you do something active.

If you are convalescing following illness or surgery, red jasper will enable you to rest and build up your reserves of strength. If you have chosen this stone you want more from your relaxation than to drift away on a cloud, for this is a stone of power, energy and true recreation.

And if you unwind best of all with some 'horizontal action', red jasper will STIMULATE your SEX-DRIVE, as well as helping you to TUNE in to your lover.

LEPIDOLITE

If you tend to go to extremes, lepidolite is a wonderful stabilizer, calming you when you are 'hyper' and encouraging you when you feel depressed. If you want to be comfortable alone, to feel the peace of your own space, this stone is for you. If you are harassed and wish to make the most of any tranquil interludes, lepidolite will help you to move smoothly into a state of calm.

It is useful for relieving the stresses of daily life and will enable you to let go of anger and frustration. You may have chosen it instinctively if you are subject to harmful emotions such as hatred (of your co-worker, for instance) or road rage. It relieves nightmares and aids psychic powers.

If you love to use your leisure time READING TAROT or doing ASTROLOGY, lepidolite is a fine companion.

PREHNITE

If you have chosen prehnite, you feel a need to change your perspective, to have a wider view of reality than the one you may feel stuck with on a day-to-day level, and to plug into a more 'cosmic consciousness'. Prehnite enhances love of Nature and the ability to use its healing influence. On a practical level, prehnite helps you to get rid of the junk that may be crowding your life and to have faith that the Universe will provide you with what you need.

Keep it by you when sorting and recycling, for a wonderful feeling of freedom. It also helps you organize your domestic space, so that harmony prevails and it becomes a haven of healing for you and your family.

This stone also CALMS irrational FEARS and HYPERACTIVITY.

RHODOCHROSITE

This dynamic stone is a wonderful support and encouragement if you like to spend your spare time in charitable pursuits. It is positive and creative, inspiring resourceful solutions and leading to delight.

Rhodocrosite will help you laugh and be warm and playful. It is a sexy stone, helping you to connect with your lover and be honest about your needs, teaching you that all your feelings are acceptable.

This is not an especially 'polite' stone, because it frees up feelings and encourages honesty, so if you are prone to use your spare time pleasing others, rhodochrosite will enable you to say 'no' pleasantly and firmly, so that you have more hours for yourself.

It is also a fine stone for any CREATIVE work such as art and craft, sculpture or anything that requires you to be PASSIONATE and FULL-BLOODED.

ROSE QUARTZ

If you have chosen rose quartz then relaxation, to you, means closeness with friends and family or romantic times with a lover. This stone will bring calm in a family crisis or in traumatic times, and it will enable you to appreciate beauty in your surroundings and in other people. It will also enhance your response to art and music.

If you have been hurt and are plagued by resentment and/or jealousy, gentle rose quartz will enable you to let go of those negative feelings, to feel warmth and affection and to prepare yourself to love again. Most important of all, rose quartz teaches you to love yourself, to count all your good qualities and to ensure that you seek the company of warm and loving souls.

It will guide you to CHOOSE CLOTHES and adornments, to make you look your BEST.

SMITHSONITE

Should you feel close to a breakdown, soothing smithsonite will help you to let go of tension and smile. If you want to relax well in the company of children, this stone will help you to relate to them by putting you in touch with your own 'inner child'. It helps you to see the ways in which your inner child may be hurt and needy, and to heal this without detriment to your relationships with others.

Life's problems seem at a distance with smithsonite; it allows you to get things into perspective. It will also help you to be tactful and to get your own way by diplomacy, so if you have a leadership role in a club, smithsonite might be your choice to oil the wheels – and get your way!

Placed beneath the bed, smithsonite BOOSTS the IMMUNE system and COMBATS alcoholism.

SUGILITE

If your work involves healing and helping people, sugilite will help you to remain positive while keeping a sense of vocation and purpose. It brings you the peace of knowing that you act by your convictions, and the relaxation in the knowledge of a benign and meaningful Universe. It is an extremely spiritual stone, bringing enlightenment and inspiration if you feel you are on an inner quest or wish to deepen your experience.

If you have been traumatized or let down, sugilite brings calm, comfort and hope. It also helps with special needs such as autism or dyslexia by connecting to the deep areas where such problems arise. If you have chosen sugilite, you may see relaxation in terms of self-development and spiritual progress. It is also good for pain relief, especially headache.

This stone will help you to OPEN out to the TRUE MEANINGS in your life.

BLUE TOURMALINE

This is an excellent stone for communication, so if you feel uptight when trying to express yourself or have a special difficulty such as a stammer, blue tourmaline will help you relax and let the words flow. Along with green tourmaline, it helps you to feel in tune with plants and is wonderful if gardening is your hobby or anything to do with growth.

If you like to use your spare time helping the environment, this stone will show the way. If you have chosen blue tourmaline, you may have a pent-up unhappiness that you need to release, or you may be helping others to do this. It is a lovely 'tea and sympathy' stone.

On a practical note, tourmaline helps you be physically COORDINATED and so SUPPORTS many ACTIVITIES, from writing to tabletennis.

FREE YOUR MIND VISUALIZATION

Many of the restrictions we experience in life are self-imposed. This visualization will help you to get a wider perspective. You may want to put this on a tape recording before you start.

1 Sit or lie comfortably and relax as described at the beginning of the chapter. Hold your Relaxation Crystal cupped in your palms or if you are lying down place it on your solar plexus (or wherever feels comfortable) with your hands gently covering it. Imagine that your crystal is radiating a force field. You may experience a tingling in your hands and body as you do this. Feel this force field forming a bubble around you. You are becoming weightless. Visualize yourself rising into the air, up, up, higher and higher.

2 Now you are drifting away, leaving behind your house and street, out over the open country. Green fields stretch beneath you, meandering rivers, woodland, hills, valleys, mountain and lakes. Drink in the colours and the landscapes.

4 You are leaving the Earth behind. There it hangs in space, a beautiful emerald orb with the moon beside it. In the distance the sun is a huge star, getting smaller as you drift into the dark reaches of the solar system. Around you there are a million stars, shining like crystals. Travel as long and as far as you like, exploring the Universe. When you are ready come back to everyday awareness, ground yourself and make notes in your notebook.

3 Now you are drifting out over the ocean. Beneath you the waves heave, blue, grey, emerald, purple. From horizon to horizon there is only water, deep peaceful water. Dusk begins to fall and the full moon appears. How marvellously it reflects on the water. You feel yourself going up higher, into the indigo sky spattered with stars and luminous with moonlight.

TENSION
SPOT
RELAXATION

If you have been practising relaxation, you will be aware of the areas of your body most prone to knots of tension. These take the longest to relax and are the first to contort if something upsets you.

1 To deal with these areas you will need your crystal in a smooth shape that feels comfortable next to your skin. Sit quietly holding your crystal and imagine that it is pulsating with healing energy.

2 When you feel ready, place it on your problem area, imagining it gently radiating calm, emanating a power that dissolves all tension, leaving behind only peace and tranquillity. If you have a partner who is also tuned in to crystals, he or she can apply the crystal and help in the visualization. You can leave your crystal in place for up to 20 minutes, although you may feel benefits much earlier. Don't forget to cleanse your crystal carefully after each anti-tension session.

ENTER YOUR CRYSTAL EXERCISE

Prepare for this exercise as you would for scrying (see 'Your Meditation Crystal'). You will need as large a specimen of your crystal as possible – a ball is ideal – so that you can get truly absorbed.

1 Become as relaxed as you can and gaze deep into the centre of your crystal. Focus your eyes on a distant point and imagine that there is a whole world inside your crystal. At this point you may choose to close your eyes the better to picture your journey. You can leave your eyes open if what you imagine is vivid enough.

2 Imagine your crystal is large, much larger than you thought. In fact, it is much bigger than you. In your mind's eye stand in front of it and admire its wonderful colours, and the subtle shapes you see within it. As you look at it you see that a door is forming. The door has a handle. Grasp the handle, open the door and enter your crystal.

3 At first it seems as if you are in a cave, with crystal walls all around you. You turn to look at the door but it has vanished. You can only wander deeper into the crystal, meandering through crystalline tunnels, illuminated by a subtle light. Ask for guidance from the crystal spirit and to be shown things that will help you in your quest for relaxation.

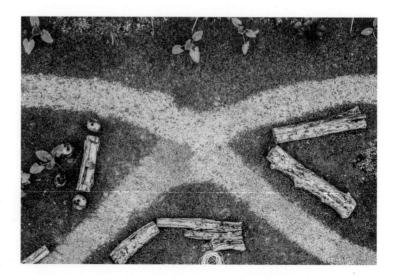

4 At this point the spirit of the crystal will come to guide you. He or she may take your hand. Now the light within the crystal is growing and the walls around you become smoother until you find yourself in a magnificent hallway, similar to a cathedral, with an atmosphere of welcome, peace and warmth.

5 Off this hallway lead many closed doors with handles. You know that in the rooms behind these doors lie important messages for you. You ask your guiding spirit to show you which one to open. Go in and explore the room, noticing all the details.

6 Within these rooms you may find a wide variety of scenes. Some will contain books, some will show games or groups of people, some will lead into peaceful gardens, some will show massage and similar therapies. This is a world of peace, tranquillity, enjoyment and blessing. Explore at your leisure and linger as you wish.

7 When the time is right, ask your guardian to lead you back to the original door. Return through the imposing hallway, into the rougher tunnel and find again the door by which you entered, materialized anew for your use. Thank your mentor and bid farewell as you return to the everyday.

8 This visualization will have shown you messages about what you need to relax. Some may not be obvious at first and some might be a surprise – for instance, you may have thought you needed to be alone and to have some peace, whereas you found yourself welcomed into one of the rooms by a laughing crowd of people. Make no assumptions until you have reflected. If you are still unsure, you can repeat the exercise as often as you wish. Note all you see in your notebook.

YOUR HEALING CRYSTAL

—

Crystals can be of great help in maintaining the inner harmony and balance that means health. True health is not merely an absence of disease, but a positive state of vitality and pleasure in life. It is important to remember that crystals cannot take the place of professional medical advice.

Few of us are free from 'dis-ease' today. Our lives are stressful and we do not take the time to listen to our bodies or to eat properly. We are bombarded by pollutants of all descriptions, from chemicals in our food to harmful radiation from the technology that surrounds us. 'Dis-ease', or a lack of easefulness and harmony, is at the root of what we know as disease. Not only our bodies, but our souls need healing, since we have cut ourselves off from our true essence, caught in the 'head stuff' of modern life. Most of us are vaguely aware that something is amiss, but are unsure exactly what.

Crystals can help redress the balance. Even if you enjoy very good physical health, you can benefit from your own special healing crystal to help you feel truly energized. Your healing crystal can help when you feel below par, such as when you think you are catching a cold, but it can also be of use when you feel run down and battered by life, when you have simply had a hard and depleting day, or have had to deal with people who drain you. Your healing crystal may also be a help if you have a talent for healing others, protecting you as you transfer healing energy.

CHOOSING YOUR HEALING CRYSTAL

Before selecting your crystal it is important to relax and to reflect on your physical, mental and spiritual health. All crystals have healing qualities, but the following have been chosen for their range of attributes.

YOU WILL NEED

Tumble-stones of the following crystals: Apache tear, amber, red sardonyx, chrysoprase, blue calcite, turquoise, black tourmaline, rhodonite, smoky quartz, malachite, purple fluorite, moonstone. Green and blue candles and cloths; lavender oil.

MEDITATION METHOD

This method is based on a feeling of optimum health. If you do not have a specific complaint or simply prefer to concentrate on feeling fantastic, this is the method for you. Lay out all the crystals before you on a cloth of green or blue. Burn a candle of the same colour if you wish, and to ensure that you relax, place a little lavender oil on your temples or heat it in a burner.

Hold your hands in your lap, next to each other, gently cupped. Turn your attention to your body and relax deeply. Now either think about a time in your life when you felt at your peak, bursting with health and vitality; or if you feel fantastic now, be extra aware of this. Feel the energy gathering in your solar plexus and spreading out, so that your whole body is radiant with it. Hold this feeling for a few moments then imagine that this feeling is being magnified and prolonged by a crystal held in your cupped hands. Which one is it?

HEALING MEDITATION METHOD

An adaptation of the previous method, try this if you wish to use your crystal primarily to heal others. Set out the crystals and settle yourself as above, visualizing a golden glow starting in your solar plexus and radiating out, similar to the previous method. This time, however, you are aware that your primary goal is to gather this energy for healing other people, plants or animals.

Ask for guidance from whatever higher power or guardian spirit you honour. Imagine that this energy is a gift that you have been given, that you are going to pass on to others, and that this gift is emanating from a crystal held in your cupped hands. Which crystal do you see with your mind's eye?

COLOUR VISUALIZATION METHOD

You don't need an actual crystal present in order to use this method on a troublesome condition that needs to be healed. The pictures of crystals in this book can be used as a focus. Simply direct your attention to the part of your body that is troubling you. What colour can you visualize soothing it? If you have a pain, what colour would you like to wrap round it. Blue or green can calm pain or itching, red or orange can revitalize while black can banish a wart or verruca. Emotional hurts may also be healed this way – for instance, disappointment might call for orange or yellow. Sit quietly, breathe deeply and see what comes into your mind. Go by your instincts. Which stone is the colour that you need?

Give yourself some time for this exercise and be aware that it could evoke difficult feelings if your pain is emotional.

INTERPRETING YOUR RELAXATION CRYSTAL

APACHE TEAR

This gentler form of black obsidian coaxes out deeply held emotions and enables the negative to be transformed into the positive. If apache tear is your choice then you may be holding on to old wounds and resentments. This may cause your body to retain toxins and may result in you feeling sluggish and not at your best.

This stone will enable you to understand what is within, to bring it to the light of day, to grieve or rage if you need to; and to let go and move on. Inhibitions can be released and your faith in yourself can be restored. With the comfort of this stone you can achieve understanding and forgiveness, especially of yourself, and so recover.

Apache tear EASES muscle TENSION, CLEANSES the body and helps vitamin absorption.

AMBER

Strictly speaking, amber is not a crystal but fossilized resin from ancient cone-bearing trees, bringing with it the riches of the earth. If you have chosen amber, you may need an injection of optimism. Depression can rob you of your physical vitality, but the heartening influence of this stone stimulates the body and encourages enthusiasm and faith in life.

Amber encourages creativity and clears the mind, so that you can build on a realistic basis to achieve your ambitions. Physically, amber relieves stress by enabling you to see a wider picture and so become balanced and cheerful. It is good for the joints and helps throat and digestive problems. It acts as a tonic for the body's cleansing system by supporting the liver, kidneys and bladder.

Amber REPELS infection and CONNECTS with the ENERGIES of the earth in order to promote healing.

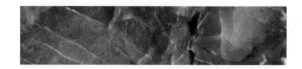

BLUE CALCITE

This stone of peace and trust has a very beneficial effect on the emotions and the nervous system. If you have chosen blue calcite, you may have been through a period of stress and trauma and need peace and rest to recuperate. Blue calcite soothes away anxieties and helps you to be clear about what you feel and why. It enables you to say what you need to say while retaining harmony and tranquillity.

Blue calcite is helpful for any mental work, dissolving blocks to creativity and conferring the strength and positive attitude that can help you overcome obstacles. It is excellent for the bones and skin, helping the immune system and soothing pain and discomfort on all levels.

Blue calcite lowers BLOOD PRESSURE and fosters TRUST in life that will enable you to draw on COSMIC ENERGIES for healing.

CHRYSOPRASE

This lovely green stone is a wonderful aid to relaxation. If you have been working so hard that you feel you are losing the plot, chrysoprase will enable you to reconnect with the true meaning of life and the beauty of the natural world. Chrysoprase reminds you of your ideals and values and enables you to let go of egotism and judgement in favour of acceptance and love of self and others. In this way it reveals fresh alternatives and encourages a relaxed openness that recognizes opportunities.

It facilitates a good night's sleep, free of nightmares, and calms phobias. If you wish to conceive, this stone can boost fertility and generally enhance the health of the sexual organs, bringing fulfilment.

Chrysoprase REGULATES the HORMONES and helps the body to EXPEL toxins.

BLACK TOURMALINE

This is a stone for strength and defence. If you have chosen black tourmaline, you may feel you are under threat or have many challenges to meet for which you will need all your resources. Black tourmaline has the power to repel attack on a psychic level and to give you the physical vitality to do whatever needs to be done on the practical side. Best of all, it enables you to keep your cool, so everything is kept in proportion and manageable.

One of this stone's most valuable uses is to protect against electromagnetic energies from computers and mobiles – for this purpose it can be worn around the neck.

Black tourmaline draws negative energy away from the body, BALANCES the brain hemispheres, helps ARTHRITIS and is beneficial for the SPINE.

PURPLE FLUORITE

A very spiritual stone, purple fluorite encourages psychic fine tuning. If you have chosen purple fluorite you may fear that you are being manipulated and invaded on a subtle level and realize that you need to shut down and protect yourself while attuning to higher states of consciousness. However, it also helps you organize your mind and environment, enabling you to scrutinize your habits and subconscious motivations and to change them if necessary.

This stone enables you to access your intuition and develop psychic gifts while retaining common sense. It will help you to heal yourself through meditation.

Fluorite is also good for INFLAMMATION, colds and NERVE PAIN and is a TONIC for sexual desires, especially if these have been dampened by disillusionment.

MALACHITE

This powerful stone needs to be used with care, so if you have chosen malachite take time to attune deeply to your intuitive reactions and limit contact with the stone until you are sure it is benefiting you. Malachite is very good at releasing negativity; if you have picked it you may badly need to cleanse yourself of something unpleasant or destructive, and to have the courage to move forwards into a totally new space. You can't kid yourself or others while under the influence of malachite and, as a result, outworn ties may be broken as strong emotions surface.

However, it is also a stone of profound empathy. Malachite heals all sexual problems (including traumas from childhood) and helps with women's problems including menstruation and childbirth.

Malachite treats GROWTHS, REPELS toxins and is good for TRAVEL SICKNESS.

MOONSTONE

This stone makes you aware of your dreams as the language of your subconscious. By getting to know yourself at a deep level you can make a new start in life. If you have chosen moonstone you may feel alienated from yourself and have lost contact with that 'still small voice' within.

Moonstone brings body wisdom, aligning the instincts with the intellect. It is a very feminine stone and can help women contact the Goddess within, or help men to find their feminine side. It encourages you to 'go with the flow' and draws out and heals the emotions, soothes the digestion and stabilizes hormones.

It helps with SHOCK and disorders such as ADHD (attention deficit hyperactivity disorder), and is particularly good for the FEMININE reproductive system.

RED SARDONYX

An excellent energy source, red sardonyx provides stimulation and encouragement in all areas of life. If you have chosen red sardonyx, you may need an infusion of élan to make a fresh assault on life, to get out of a rut, achieve a cherished ambition and to strengthen your willpower. Red sardonyx will give you vitality but it will also help you to exercise control and draw on your deepest wells of stamina.

It is a stone of decision and determination, attracting good fortune through a positive attitude. This stone also confers protection by helping you to be true to yourself. It helps you attract partners that complement you and bring you joy. It sharpens all the senses.

Red sardonyx is a STIMULANT to the metabolism, also helping the LUNGS and IMMUNE system.

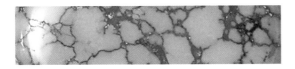

TURQUOISE

Lovely turquoise helps you to see how beautiful life is even at its simplest, and encourages you to count your blessings. If you have chosen turquoise you may have become self-pitying and have turned into your own worst enemy. This stone will enable you to be calm and positive, and to find things that bring you joy and release creativity.

Turquoise alleviates panic attacks and fears of speaking in public and protects against pollution from the environment. It is a friend in times of exhaustion or depletion from environmental causes. Because it confers serenity it creates the right state of mind for making romantic contacts and for having fun. Laughter – a great tonic to the immune system – is more readily provoked with this stone.

Physically, turquoise SOOTHES inflammation, STIMULATES the absorption of nutrients and FIGHTS infection.

SMOKY QUARTZ

This stone forms a powerful connection to the earth and so aids in grounding and stabilizing. It is important to be sure the stone is natural, not irradiated. If you have chosen smoky quartz you may feel you are going through a period of unavoidable difficulty and need a steady stream of supportive energy to help you through. Smoky quartz will calm your fears and help you to take each day as it comes, finding comfort and enjoyment in day-to-day things.

It helps concentration and practicality, and in the end will guide you towards the realization of your dreams. Physically it helps increase tolerance levels, eases headaches, generally stimulates, strengthens and encourages the body to absorb minerals.

Smoky quartz is good for the REPRODUCTIVE organs, MUSCLES, nerves and HEART.

RHODONITE

This stone of warmth and harmony carries the message that love is the greatest healing force of all. If you have chosen rhodonite you may feel you have suffered through coldness – either your own or the coldness of others – and that you want to be able to open out, to give, to make contact and be positive.

Rhodonite can connect you to the healing and nurturing powers of a community, enabling you to take without guilt and give without counting the cost. It heals abuse and destructive relationship patterns, encourages the release of emotions, responsibility and true forgiveness. Best of all, it promotes healthy self-love that enables you truly to love others. It is excellent for trauma and extreme emotional states.

Rhodonite is good for the HEARING, for healing WOUNDS and bites, and for boosting FERTILITY.

SOUL HEALING MEDITATION

Wounds to the soul can occur in childhood due to trauma or abuse, or can be from a past life. These wounds interfere with growth and stop us having the harmonious relationship with the world that is our birthright. Soul healing may be a deep matter, but with the aid of your crystal it is possible to make a start.

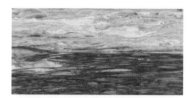

1 Make sure your surroundings feel safe and that you will not be disturbed. Cover yourself with a green shawl (or any colour that feels right) and lie down holding your crystal over your heart.

2 Try to relax and ask to be taken back in time to when the trauma occurred. Do not worry if this image does not come to you clearly. You can simply imagine yourself as a small child who is hurt, or a wounded adult if your intuition suggests past-life involvement. When you have this image in your mind, send love and compassion to this person and imagine your crystal growing larger and larger, wrapping itself around the hurt person like a glowing bubble. Within this chamber of love and peace, the wounds are being healed; see the person becoming whole and happy.

3 You may need to do this a number of times before you feel it is complete. After each session, give thanks, cleanse your crystal, take a drink of spring water and make note of all that has occurred in your notebook.

HEALING OTHERS RITUAL

Many people – perhaps all of us – are able to transfer healing energies to those who need them. Crystals can certainly help. All healing should only be done with the consent and co-operation of the person being healed, otherwise it is an infringement of boundaries or even an ego-trip.

1 Try to obtain a clear quartz wand – natural or shaped – to use in addition to your healing crystal, but if this is not possible, use your fingers to direct the energy instead. Whenever you are healing ask for guidance from the higher power or force you believe in and to be aware that the energy you are channelling is not the property of your own ego but comes from the cosmos.

2 Face the person and hold your healing crystal close to your abdomen with your passive hand. Affirm that you are drawing energy within you. Feel it flowing up through your legs from the earth, and gathering in your solar plexus. Feel light drawing down from above through the crown of your head, meeting the other energy-source within you. Feel your crystal amplifying this energy and be aware of it as a golden glow.

3 Hold your quartz wand in your active hand, direct this energy into your arm and down into the wand. Point the wand at the part of the body to be healed and imagine a stream of light entering it from the wand, healing all hurts. When you have finished, consciously close yourself off from external energy, eat and drink something, and cleanse both your crystal and the quartz wand. Make notes about your experience in your notebook.

FERTILITY-BOOSTING RITUAL

If you are trying for a child, your healing crystal can help you to enhance your fertility. This simple ritual will get through to your subconscious, which influences the body in subtle ways.

1 Place the lilies in moonlight for a night, if possible. Next evening, place the crystal tumble-stone in the egg cup and gently stroke some pollen from the lilies onto the stone (be careful, the pollen stains).

2 Heat the jasmine oil in a burner (this will be unnecessary if the lilies are heavily scented) and light the candle. Place your egg cup in front of the candle and imagine your fertility and swelling within you. Imagine a baby growing and coming into your life. Hold these images for as long as you like, developing and extending them.

3 Cover the egg cup with the cloth and place it under or beside your bed. This exercise can be repeated monthly; simply cleanse the crystal in a running stream, wash out the egg cup and obtain more lilies. The white candle may be relit as often as necessary. If lilies are hard to find, any flower with plentiful pollen may be used but white is the best colour.

YOU WILL NEED

Your healing crystal in the form of a tumble-stone; an egg cup, a white candle, some lilies (preferably growing in a pot), a small white cloth, some jasmine oil and a tiny brush.

PHYSICAL HEALING VISUALIZATION

Your healing crystal can help with any bodily problem; the simplest way is by direct contact with the skin. If you have pain in any part of your body, place the crystal as close to the pain as you can. Visualize the colour of the crystal bathing the area, taking away all the discomfort. Hold this image for as long as you can and you should gain significant relief.

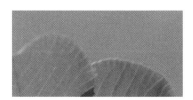

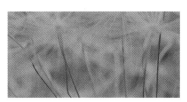

1 Lie comfortably with your crystal close by. Imagine the spirit of the crystal emerging from within, growing to human size and standing beside you. Now imagine this spirit ministering to you. You may ask for advice if you wish and you may 'hear' the answer within your mind. When the time feels right, thank your crystal spirit before you say goodbye.

2 Alternatively, you may place your crystal in pure spring water for an hour or so, in order that the water may absorb some of the crystal's energies. You may then dab the energized water on any affected areas of your body.

Another healing method concerns the spirit of your crystal and is more subtle. Use it for problems that are vague, general or internal, such as tiredness or depression, or for something like diabetes, high blood pressure or weight loss. (Please note that using your crystal should not take the place of medical care, and if you have, or suspect you have a serious condition, you should consult a health professional without delay.)

YOUR
LOVE
CRYSTAL

—

Love is top of the list of 'wants' for most of us. We all need to be needed, we all want to feel part of something warm and close. However, there are many barriers to love. These may come from early conditioning and experiences or simply from expectations that are too high, shyness or fear.

In our times we enjoy a great deal of freedom when it comes to choosing a partner, and we are in a position to decide very firmly what will and will not do. But with freedom comes responsibility, and with choice may come disappointment, as it may be very difficult for reality to match up to the fantasy we have fixed upon.

Your Love Crystal will help you to deal with important issues and dissolve the barriers that come between you and the love and closeness you desire. In addition, it can help you overcome the two greatest and simplest obstacles of all. The first of these concerns loving yourself. Unless you love yourself, unless you have self-esteem, self-worth, you will find it very hard to attract someone who truly loves and respects you, because you are just not giving out the right 'vibes'. The second concerns the ability to love. Can you open your heart? Can you feel true empathy and give of yourself? In order to have a lover, you need to be a lover. In the game of love the stakes can be high – your Love Crystal will weight the dice in your favour and so find the love and fulfilment you need.

CHOOSING YOUR LOVE CRYSTAL

Many crystals are connected to love in some form or fashion, but some are especially appropriate. The following have been selected for their links to love. Some – especially diamond – may be quite expensive, but if you cannot purchase all of the stones in raw or tumble-stone form, maybe you could borrow some in jewellery from a friend, buying for yourself the one that turns out to be 'yours'.

YOU WILL NEED

Choose from rose quartz, amber, lapis lazuli, ruby, emerald, diamond, sapphire, angelite, amethyst, brown agate, golden calcite and hematite. Rose- or pink-coloured cloths and candles; rose petals.

THE MEDITATION METHOD

This method is more general than method two and may serve if you are older and experienced, and have memories that are less than happy.

Start by laying out the crystals before you on a rose- or pink-coloured cloth and burn a candle of the same colour. Sprinkle pink or red rose petals around the crystals. Sit in front of the crystals feeling relaxed and harmonious. If you have some memories you prefer not to recall, allow your mind to focus on something uplifting, such as a beautiful tree or flower; there is no need to think about any specific human love. Relax until you are able to think positively and be kind to yourself. Allow a sensation of warmth and openness to begin in your chest. Slowly feel it expanding, wider and wider, taking in the whole world in joy and love. Be aware of all the wonderful things that surround you. When you are ready, let your attention come back to the crystals. Which one best fits this glow in your heart?

At the end of this ritual it is very important that you close down your subtle senses, so imagine your heart closing up, like the petals of a wonderful flower, folding back into a tight bud. Eat and drink something and pat your body, to affirm that you are 'back'.

This ritual involves you opening yourself up, so it is important not to leave yourself vulnerable. You should feel encouraged and filled with faith in your crystal.

THE ROSE VISUALIZATION METHOD

If you have been able to obtain all of the crystals, lay them out before you on a rose- or pink-coloured cloth and burn a candle of the same colour. Sprinkle pink or red rose petals around the crystals. Clear quartz may be substituted for diamond (but if diamond turns out to be your choice you will need to obtain the real thing). If you do not have the crystals, you may use substitutes, such as names written on coloured paper or glass beads of the correct colour. However, because love is so strong an emotion, it may be possible to make your choice with no actual crystals present – the choice may just arrive in your mind as you do the visualization.

Close your eyes and relax, allowing your mind to go into a dreamy state. Now think of a time when you felt really, truly loved and treasured, or simply a time when you felt confident of your lovability. Or think of a time when you felt love, very strongly and deeply, for another person. Which stone fits that feeling? Your eyes may open and alight upon a stone or you may just 'know' deep inside.

The drawback with this method may be that it harks back to a former ruptured relationship, to a ring you had or some other memento. If so, try the meditation method.

INTERPRETING YOUR LOVE CRYSTAL

ROSE QUARTZ

One of the most truly loving crystals of all, rose quartz brings peace, acceptance, healing and affection. If you have chosen rose quartz, your heart may need to be soothed after a broken romance or you need to be able to trust once more. This stone will help you forgive yourself and release old patterns that are keeping you from love – it enables repressed emotions to be released so that you can move onwards.

Of course, it is also possible that you have chosen this stone because you have a great deal of love within you to give to others. So great are its loving powers that you may find wearing it draws more attention your way than you can handle.

Rose quartz will help you to EMPATHIZE and to RECEIVE UNDERSTANDING.

AMBER

Not really a stone but tree-resin, amber brings with it the vibrant life force of the earth. If you have chosen amber you may need to have your faith in love restored in order to be enthusiastic about relationships and to be able to see the best in others. Amber empowers you to make the best of

yourself and to exude warmth and responsiveness; it has been used through the ages to enhance beauty and sex appeal and to dispel loneliness.

It increases fertility and sexual prowess. This gem also helps to increase sensual pleasure and abandonment by its link with the powers of the natural world. Worn near the heart it has the power to attract a mate.

Amber brings HAPPINESS at all levels but especially in the REALM of RELATIONSHIPS.

AMETHYST

This very spiritual and tranquil stone brings contact with higher realms yet also helps with common sense. If you have chosen amethyst you may wish to connect with another at a very deep level, and you may desire to be uplifted and inspired. Possibly you feel that past relationships have been too focused on the material or you may simply be most at home on the spiritual plane, which does not mean you lack sensuality but that you see the body as a vehicle for spirit.

It calms self-destructive passions and addictive behaviour patterns. Amethyst can show you another reality without encouraging self-deception. It is a stone of unconditional love and may awaken psychic senses, so that you 'know' how others feel.

Traditionally, amethyst was EXCHANGED by LOVERS to signify COMMITMENT.

BROWN AGATE

Agate has a stabilizing and strengthening effect, encouraging inner balance. If you have chosen agate as your Love Crystal you may need to be honest with yourself about your feelings. Pent-up negative emotions such as spite and jealousy can keep you from attracting love, since others may be aware of this at an instinctive level.

Agate heals, helps you to feel safe and relaxes you to accept yourself as you are and so receive love. Of course, you may also have chosen agate because you are level-headed and sensible, and wish to enhance this. Agate has long been used in love-spells, to draw on the bounty of the Earth.

This stone helps you to find PRACTICAL solutions in matters to do with love, relationships and generally ATTRACTING a MATE.

LAPIS LAZULI

This lovely blue stone is very powerful, having ancient associations with royalty and with the goddess Isis. It can help you express yourself with confidence and dignity. If you have chosen lapis lazuli you may have had experiences in the past that made you feel demeaned, and you now wish to

enhance your self-worth. It may also mean that your priority in relationships is a sense of self-respect, pride and fulfilment.

Lapis lazuli ensures dignity, equality and true communication. It also helps the psychic powers, enabling you to tune in to the needs and feelings of others, if you so wish. It has long been considered a fidelity charm and lovers may wear it to strengthen the bonds between them.

In general, this stone brings peace and a LOVE that UNITES the physical, mental, emotional and spiritual LEVELS.

RUBY

Polished ruby is expensive but it is possible to get uncut stones. This rich red stone comes replete with energy and passion. If you have chosen ruby it is likely that you want to liven up your social life and have lots of sex. You may also desire a passionate love affair that involves you deeply, with lots of physical expression and extravagant romance.

However, if you tend to be a bit hyperactive, ruby can have a calming effect on you, helping you to focus on what you feel and do. Ruby jewellery has long been worn to drive out sadness and to attract riches of all descriptions.

Ruby confers a LUST for LIFE, and gives you COURAGE when meeting new people or going out on dates.

SAPPHIRE

Pure blue sapphire is a spiritual stone that reveals the truth and brings clarity. You may have chosen sapphire if you have been confused about a relationship and about what you want from love, or your ability to be lovable and loving (or indeed whether you truly want love at all). You may also be drawn to sapphire if you want honesty and open communication in a relationship above all things and to share similar ideals.

Sapphire brings peace and fidelity, a 'meeting of true minds'. It was once used to ensure chastity, but this may also be taken to mean a restriction of sexual activity to a committed partner.

This stone GUARDS love from any THREAT, internal or external, and oils the wheels socially, so that romantic CONTACTS can be made.

DIAMOND

Although this stone is now a favourite for engagement rings, its association with love is fairly recent. The diamond's brilliance is also of fairly recent origin, following the discovery that pressure on the correct point allows the stone to be cut into many facets. Diamonds are wonderful for enhancing self-confidence with the opposite sex, and if you need a boost in this, you may well be drawn to diamond. However, this scintillating stone is a natural choice if you are an extravert and relish being the centre of attention.

Diamond increases energy at all levels and cuts through any deception or murkiness, so you cannot kid yourself or be content with second best. It brings a clear expression of needs and feelings and gives you the courage to tackle difficult issues. This stone has long been linked with abundance.

Diamonds HEAL quarrels and ensure FIDELITY between LOVERS.

EMERALD

The brilliant green of emerald is representative of our planet Earth and all her riches. For eons, wearing an emerald close to your heart has been used as a way of attracting a lover. If you have chosen emerald, you may have been through a bad time and need the strength to overcome this but also to count the good things you do have, to amplify them and enjoy them to the full.

Emerald's loving influence facilitates setting up home with your lover. This stone helps understanding and wisdom, but it also brings material benefits so that the marriage bed may be filled with delights and the table laden with good food.

Emerald ensures that lovers will also be friends, and brings the PATIENCE to RESOLVE issues and establish SECURITY.

ANGELITE

This blue-white stone is very much in keeping with the New Age and its message of human brother- and sisterhood. If you have chosen angelite your ideas and wishes with regard to relationships may be unconventional. You may possibly like an 'open' type of relationship where you are principally a friend to your lover, or have several relationships which you conduct in a broad-minded, honest and relaxed fashion. Maybe you do not particularly want demands or involvement, but prefer affection and friendliness with all. Or it may be that you seek a true spiritual bonding.

There is much compassion and peace with this stone. If you have had bad experiences of intimacy it will enable you to interact with warmth, remaining self-contained and yet totally honest with yourself and others about your motives and feelings.

It is a good stone to facilitate TELEPATHIC COMMUNICATION between LOVERS.

GOLDEN CALCITE

This cleansing, clearing stone amplifies energies. If this is your choice you may feel emotionally contaminated and that the loves you have had have been grounded in unhealthy patterns or cravings. Golden calcite helps you to use your emotional intelligence and to fall in love with your head as well as your heart. It will harmonize with you if you prefer to have your head rule your heart, enabling both sides to have their say.

Calcite prevents you from getting carried away, at the same time magnifying positive energy, keeping you quick-witted and resourceful. It enables you to trust your judgement in love matters. Calcite encourages fair and mature relationships, but it is also good for flirting and fun.

It brings lightness, BRIGHTNESS and OPPORTUNITIES for creating a loving future, filled with creative POTENTIAL.

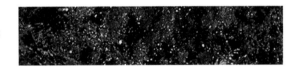

HEMATITE

This silvery-black stone is a powerful grounder and protector. If you have chosen it you may want to come down to earth after a relationship that involved illusion or deception – including self-deception – or you may want to be emotionally or physically protected. It helps overcome sexual cravings and it strengthens willpower and courage. It is a good friend if involved in the legalities of divorce, but on a positive note it helps you to make the most of your assets and to enhance your sex appeal in a very earthy way.

Because it draws attention and consciousness very much into the physical, it can aid orgasm. When bonding with a lover it enables you to focus on each other's creature comforts, strengthening the sensual bonds that are between you.

Hematite PROTECTS any commitment made from OUTSIDE interference and brings COMFORT and closeness.

LOVING YOURSELF EXERCISE

To attract the love of another person, the first requirement is to love yourself; unless you truly believe you are lovable it is hard to radiate that magnetic confidence. Your crystal can help you attain that inner glow.

1 Do this exercise in the bath. Choose bath salts or oils to coordinate with the colour of your crystal and place as many candles as you like of the same colour in the bathroom. Make sure the bathroom is warm and that you have a snuggly towel and soothing lotion for after-bath pampering. Place your love crystal where you can see it while you are in the bath, and surround it with candles. If possible have more than one crystal. However, to be on the safe side do not place your crystal in the bath, for some oils can have a detrimental effect on some crystals.

2 Rub the bathwater gently and sensually all over your body, saying 'Feet, I love you. Legs, I love you', continuing until you have covered your whole body with love. Imagine all the good things that part of your body does. Visualize yourself glowing with the power of your crystal. Concentrate on your positive attributes, feel warm, imagine compliments, embraces, caresses and pampering.

3 When you are ready leave your bath, towel dry, rub in lotion (repeating self-loving affirmations) and give yourself a treat such as a glass of wine or some chocolate. If you experienced any difficulties, note these in your crystal notebook. You can repeat this exercise as often as you like.

ATTRACTING LOVE RITUAL

The essence of your crystal can help you draw towards yourself the love that you want.

1 Find the narrowest glass you have, such as a liqueur glass or jam jar and place your crystal at the bottom of this. Place the narrow glass in a much larger bowl, glass or jug and pour still spring water into the larger vessel so that it comes close to the top of the smaller glass without overflowing into it. (It is better to do this than to place the crystal directly into water as some crystals are friable or toxic.)

2 Place the bowl on the windowsill on a sunny day so that it absorbs sunlight for most of the day. If you are able to time this exercise for the full moon, follow this by placing it in moonlight for a similar span of time. If the weather is cloudy and you wish to do this without delay, wait until the evening and light a big, thick orange or gold candle and leave the crystal in the candlelight for as many hours as you can. Affirm that the energies of your crystal are being magnified and radiating out into the water in the surrounding bowl.

3 Now place the charged gem-water in a sterilized bottle. Before going out on a date or hoping to meet a lover, sip a little of the elixir, feel it entering your body with warmth and power and affirm that you radiate magnetism and the glow of your crystal. Imagine the radiance surrounding you, drawing love to you. You may dab the elixir over your body, behind your ears or on more intimate parts. To keep the elixir for more than a week, add half vodka or brandy, but avoid putting this on sensitive areas as alcohol can irritate the skin.

YOU WILL NEED

Narrow glass; larger glass bowl or jug; orange or gold candle; vodka or brandy.

OPEN YOUR HEART VISUALIZATION

If you have been hurt or disillusioned, you may close your heart; despite the fact that you consciously want to draw love towards you, unconsciously you may be giving off signals that say 'keep out'.

1 Before this visualization be honest and ask yourself if you are creating a blockage. Do you truly want to attract a lover? Maybe you just want to have a little more trust, enjoyment and fun in life. Try to sort out what you really want. Lie down where you will not be disturbed and place your crystal on your heart. Breathe steadily and allow yourself to feel relaxed and peaceful.

2 Now feel a glow starting in your chest, where your crystal is. Regardless of the colour of your crystal, imagine this glow as a wonderful shimmering green. Feel this glow extending, going outwards into the world. Feel love for all things, all the plants and animals that are on the Earth, all the people that inhabit it. Think of beautiful things – majestic trees, panoramic views, blossom, sunshine, sun-kissed waves and a feeling of joy pervading all.

3 When you are ready to come back to everyday awareness, ground yourself by closing down your subtle senses; imagine your heart closing up like the petals of a flower. Eat and drink something and pat your body, to affirm that you are 'back'. Light a joss stick as an offering to whatever cosmic power you believe in, giving thanks for the experience. Make a note of any revelations you have.

LOVERS' BOND RITUAL

This little rite affirms the bonds between you and is a simple, yet powerful way to express love and commitment.

1 Discuss choice of crystal with your lover – is he or she happy to receive your crystal? Amethyst or rose quartz are the best choices for this exercise. Begin by honestly telling your lover about anything you are not quite happy with in the relationship. Be prepared to hear similar things in return and try to negotiate changes. Then write down all the things you love about your lover and tie it up in a scroll with the ribbon. Don't forget to list the small things they have done, like making you a morning cup of tea, as well as the big things. Exchange scrolls and love crystals with your lover.

2 Now plant the seeds carefully in the compost-tray in a shape of your choosing, maybe your initials, a heart or circle. Tend the seeds together and when the cress has grown make sure you eat it together. It is a good idea to water the cress with some gem elixir made by the method described in 'Attracting Love Ritual' (see page 83).

3 To keep your relationship vibrant and flourishing, repeat this little ritual each year, preferably at some date significant to you or at one of the equinoxes or solstices.

YOU WILL NEED

Some seeds (cress is a good choice), some compost in a tray, two sheets of paper, two pens, two ribbons, a love crystal for each of you and the cooperation of your lover.

YOUR
SUCCESS
CRYSTAL

—

Success means different things to different people, and your own definition of 'success' may well vary greatly throughout your life, depending on times and situations.

In terms of your life as a whole, the meaning of success may change radically as you grow older. At some point in your life, success may be defined as 'victory' – overcoming all odds, passing exams, getting promotion, while at another point success may be a much deeper matter of fulfilment, creativity and self-development.

While all crystals can help in self-development, your choice of the best crystal for you may change many times, and you may decide you need more than one at a time, for different purposes. This is not so much about the crystals having very different properties individually (although they vary naturally), so much as facilitating different states in you.

To find true 'success' it is helpful to be flexible and open-minded. You may find that your crystal stimulates ideas not only about how to attain your goals, but also how to formulate them.

CHOOSING YOUR SUCCESS CRYSTAL

Because your own definition of success will change, depending on your circumstances, it is preferable to obtain all the crystals as tumble-stones or very small pieces, if possible. You may find that each one has its day.

YOU WILL NEED

Crystals to choose from include tiger's eye, dendritic (tree) agate, carnelian, holey stone, aventurine, citrine, hematite, green jasper, lepidolite, sodalite, sunstone, topaz. Cinnamon sticks, green or gold cloths and candles, cinnamon oil or joss stick. Fireworks, powdered ginger.

MEDITATION METHOD

Spread the cinnamon sticks on a green or gold cloth, with the candles behind them; on the bed of cinnamon, lay out your selection of crystals, or their representation, on separate squares of paper. Burn a cinnamon joss stick or heat cinnamon oil, for good measure. Cinnamon is traditionally associated with prosperity and success.

Now relax deeply with your eyes closed. Think of a time when you were really successful, when you felt as if you had the world at your feet, riding high, exultant. Fill yourself with this feeling. When you feel as 'successful' as possible, hold your left hand (or your right, if you are left-handed) over the crystals. Keep your eyes closed, retaining the feeling and pass your hand slowly back and forth over the stones.

Note the sensations in your hand – does it feel hot or tingly, heavy or light? Is there a place where it feels most comfortable or to which it is drawn? This is the place in the line-up where you will find your Success Crystal. If you are not quite sure which crystal is indicated, remove the definite noes and keep going until you have made the final choice.

VISUALIZATION METHOD ONE

The above method assumes that at some time you have felt very successful, but this may not yet have happened to you in the way you want. However, are you able to visualize feeling really supreme? If so, just imagine what it will be like when you are truly successful in the way you want to be and proceed as above.

VISUALIZATION METHOD TWO

This method is similar to the one above, but applies to some specific challenge at which you wish to succeed. If you are choosing your crystal for this you may need to choose again when the challenge is behind you, in order to find a crystal for more general success.

Imagine that you have succeeded at the challenge – for instance, passed an exam or won a race. Please do not imagine the specifics of the effort such as revising and writing reams or running like mad. Imagine instead the certificate, the trophy, the feeling of triumph and then proceed as in the first method above.

FIREWORKS METHOD

This little ritual is really for victory, but you can use it to choose your crystal if you truly need some help from the gods for a mega challenge, such as climbing K2 or getting elected to high office. You will need a rocket or other firework that shoots upwards and sends sparks, some powdered ginger (traditionally associated with great energy and power) and your crystals (or their substitutes) in a bag.

Place a little ginger on your tongue (if you can bear it) and on your fingertips. Imagine the fruits of your success (not the process and the effort, just the fabulous result). Light the rocket and as it shoots upwards say 'I am a winner! Like the rocket, I'm unstoppable!' several times. Place a little more ginger on your fingertips and reach into your bag, pulling out the very crystal to support you on the road to victory.

Once you have your Success Crystal, you can repeat the exercise with the rocket while holding your special crystal to give the ritual more oomph and aid your powers of visualization.

INTERPRETING YOUR SUCCESS CRYSTAL

DENDRITIC AGATE

In general agate teaches self-reliance and self-value. It prevents you wasting energy envying and competing with others, and encourages you to understand your uniqueness. Dendritic agate has strong links with the earth and enables you to live in the present, valuing and experiencing each moment. If you have chosen dendritic agate, you may need to feel connected to your roots in order to discover your true path in life.

Dendritic agate brings stability and works slowly to help you find yourself. It creates peace and has very strong connections with the plant kingdom and nature spirits, so if you are looking for inspiration about your vocation, quiet time outdoors will clear your mind.

Dendritic agate will give you the strength to PERSEVERE, to see mistakes as learning EXPERIENCES and to PROGRESS.

AVENTURINE

This is a stone for good, old-fashioned luck. If you have chosen it then you may be aware that the time has come for you to cast your fate to the wind and take a chance. Aventurine will enable you to be in the right state of mind to notice opportunities and simply to play with life to see what it brings. It may bring you a whole new set of circumstances and ideas or a new way of looking at the ones you've got. It may even bring you to the crock of gold. If you have any neuroses or nervous mannerisms, aventurine will enable you to understand what has caused them and to feel relaxed enough to leave them behind.

Aventurine will enable you to INSPIRE OTHERS and to be a LEADER, if that is what you want.

CARNELIAN

This very strong stone carries vitality and courage. If you have chosen carnelian then you are either feeling extremely ambitious and very determined to compete and succeed, or you are aware that you are going to be facing some tough challenges and that you need all the help you can get!

Carnelian will help you to draw on your deepest reserves and yet still have something left. It will also help you to target your efforts, laser-like, where they will have most effect. Carnelian makes your mind crystal clear, so you can formulate realistic goals and make your choices in life in a positive and empowered fashion.

Should you be feeling apathetic and despondent, this stone is just the TONIC you need to HELP you see that better things are POSSIBLE.

CITRINE

Citrine is a wonderful stone for making a new start. It will draw out your versatility and powers of invention, helping you to reinvent yourself and your life. It will toughen you against criticism and enable you to break the mould, to express your individuality and creativity. It is a stone of fun and bright ideas. If you have chosen it you may feel stuck in a rut, needing a shove in a new direction.

This stone sharpens your mind and enables you to tell other people what you think, how you feel and what you want. Because it is stabilizing to the mind it empowers you to take responsibility.

With citrine as your guide you will be prepared to EXPLORE and leave no stone unturned in your SEARCH for success and FULFILMENT.

HEMATITE

This is a stone for survivors. If it is your choice then you may feel that you have come through a very hard time. In fact, your whole life may have been shadowed and you could feel repressed. The time has come to end all that and to go back to basics, to count your assets, your health and to start building slowly and steadily. For the moment success to you may be a matter of the practical and earthly and you are prepared to work hard and even be a little ruthless.

Hematite will show you what is driving you and can help you to HARMONIZE your SPIRIT with your BODY for more total fulfilment.

HOLEY STONE

A 'holey stone' is not truly a crystal, but as the name says, a stone that has a naturally formed hole, caused by wind, wave, soil erosion, tiny creatures or any other means. Such stones can often be found on beaches and they can also be bought in New Age shops, along with crystals.

Because of the womb symbolism they are sacred to the Great Mother and have long been considered highly protective. If you have chosen holey stone then you may be realizing that your fulfilment lies in nurturing. Maybe you are trying to bring something to birth – if so this stone will support you. Possibly you are wishing to intensify your links with the Earth and the Eternal Feminine offered by this stone.

Holey stone will help you ACCESS the riches of your UNCONSCIOUS mind, to free up creativity and ACT from the heart.

GREEN JASPER

This is a stone of balance and cooperation. It encourages discussion and helpfulness between the members of a community and helps you to understand where you have become lopsided, and helps correct this. If you have chosen green jasper, you may feel that your life is lacking in some respect and that you have lost contact with your soul.

This stone will help you find the missing parts of yourself, so that you feel whole. You may need to work less, play more, do active things if you have been office-bound, use your hands if you have been 'in the head' and so on. Green jasper helps in self-realization and healthy self-love.

If you see SUCCESS in terms of being WELL ROUNDED, in loving and being loved by all, then green jasper is your friend.

LEPIDOLITE

Purple lepidolite is a spiritual stone and if you have chosen it then it is unlikely that you define your success in physical, practical terms, but in terms of your development as a human being and your enlightenment. Maybe you wish to help others but it is not the kudos that motivates you but the feeling of being a meaningful part of the cosmos.

This calming stone will stabilize your moods so you are better able to tune in to your life path. It will enable you to cut to the chase, dispensing with distractions and make important decisions. It will also help you succeed without the help of other people, whatever the undertaking.

Although it is SPIRITUAL, it will attract LUCK, and can bring REVELATIONS about your creative fulfilment in dreams.

SODALITE

This veined blue stone resembles lapis lazuli in appearance and brings gifts of intuition and spirituality. If you have chosen sodalite, your aspirations may be abstract. Possibly you long for success in some form of higher study, or maybe you are learning a subtle skill such as healing or psychism. Sodalite keeps your logical mind in contact with your intuition so both prosper.

It is an idealistic stone for those who measure success in terms of being true to themselves and doing good. If you are planning charitable work, group sessions of some kind or teaching, sodalite will facilitate clear communication and an impeccable reputation. It enables you to inspire trust while also drawing the supportive presence of people of integrity.

Sodalite OPENS your MENTAL horizons and helps you UNDERSTAND many things, especially yourself.

SUNSTONE

As the name suggests, this stone is for those who want to shine, to bask in the limelight. If you have chosen this stone then the chances are you want to see your name up in lights. Sunstone will remove inhibitions and free you from those who would hold you back, allowing your true self to shine through. It will also help you to stop making excuses and really go for what you want.

It strengthens you so that you can say 'no' when this is necessary. Sunstone will give you inexhaustible physical energy when you are doing something creative or promoting yourself. However, it also reminds you to nurture yourself as the wonderful creature that you are.

Sunstone ENCOURAGES you to see the POSITIVE side and to turn disadvantage to ADVANTAGE.

TIGER'S EYE

This is a wonderful stone for energy, courage and luck. Its brown-yellow hues bring together the fire of the sun and the solidity of the Earth. If you have chosen tiger's eye then the chances are you are very ambitious but also aware that you must not overreach yourself.

This stone will help you keep your feet on the ground while you aim for the stars. Tiger's eye was traditionally carried as a talisman against ill-wishing and it will help you to be aware of anyone who is likely to do you harm and enable you to deal with them, bravely, firmly and sensibly. This stone will enable you to decide what you really need and what is just pie in the sky.

Tiger's eye helps you to NOTICE all RELEVANT data and to BRING the strands together.

TOPAZ

Vibrant topaz lights up the path of life and gives optimism and encouragement. If you have chosen topaz you are probably aware of the need for positive thinking. This stone will add power to your visualizations and affirmations and help you believe in yourself.

Topaz will also help you to value yourself and to realize just what you have to offer other people, so it supports confidence. It is also a very creative and artistic influence. If you have goals that are not quite formed in your mind topaz will help make them clear. It has the wonderful ability to enable you to see both the wood and the trees, and to see how they knit together.

The greatest gift of topaz is to REVEAL your abundant INNER RESOURCES, to delight in them and to use them.

ATTRACTING LUCK RITUAL

The best way to attract luck is a positive attitude and a happy outlook. Research shows that 'lucky' people are cheerful and outgoing individuals who chat to the millionaire in the taxi queue and get offered a plum job, or find money on the street. This ritual will help you 'feel' lucky. You can have an abundance of life's goodies – believe this is so and what you want will flow towards you. This is no great mystery, for if you change your consciousness and your beliefs, without realizing it you will begin to behave slightly differently. Gradually, you will attract wealth.

1 The horseshoe has long been considered a sign of luck – arrange seven of the tumble-stones in a horseshoe (or use a real horseshoe), place the eighth in the 'cup' of the horseshoe with the candle above it. Heat orange oil in an oil burner, for its optimistic 'vibes'.

2 Look at the candle flame and imagine all sorts of lucky things happening to you – meeting people, winning prizes, finding things. If big things seem too far-fetched, then just imagine small pieces of good fortune, such as finding what you want when you shop or getting a parking space. Let a big smile come over your face. Repeat 'I am lucky, lucky, lucky!' as often as you wish.

3 Carry the eighth stone with you whenever you need a dose of luck. Leave the other seven crystals as ornaments if you wish, ready to recharge your luck crystal as often as you like. Cleanse all eight crystals if you start to think negatively and begin again.

BOOST YOUR CONFIDENCE RITUAL

Confidence comes from being relaxed and having healthy self-esteem. This exercise will remind you that you are special and can achieve your goals.

YOU WILL NEED

A gold candle; a gold dish and any item of jewellery with your special crystal on it; orange oil.

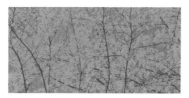

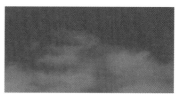

1 Place the jewellery on the gold plate and put the candle in the centre, with the jewellery near the bottom of the candle. As you light it, say 'I shine bright as this flame.'

2 Touch your fingertips to the gold plate. Concentrate on your head. Feel a shining crown placed there, dazzlingly bright, so that all of your being is radiant. Feel it drawing you upwards, so that your spine is straight. The radiance is going into your head, so your mind is bright and clear. Imagine yourself walking into a room, head held high, surrounded by this glow. Do not imagine scary scenarios in detail, now is not the time to confront them; now is the time to glow.

3 When you feel you have finished, wear your crystal and raise it to your head when you need to as a reminder that your 'crown' is in place. If you need a boost, go off into a quiet place, hold your crystal on the top of your head and strongly imagine the crown glowing there.

VOCATION MEDITATION

Although things may be fine in life, you may feel there is 'something missing'. Maybe you do not feel fulfilled. Perhaps you have the sneaking suspicion that you are capable of more. When you are busy it can be very hard to stop and take stock, but help is at hand with your crystal.

1 For this exercise you want to enter a 'dreamy' state, the better to access your unconscious. Heat some jasmine oil in a burner and sit holding your crystal – this will be better with a sizeable crystal shaped as a ball or egg. Relax deeply. Ask yourself what it is about your job or lifestyle that does not satisfy you. Give yourself time to be as clear as possible. Write all that occurs to you in your notebook.

2 Still sitting, ask yourself what you would really like to experience in your job or life. Give yourself time. There is no need to try to force a false certainty – if your ideas are unformed, leave them that way for now. Write down what you feel in your notebook.

3 Now lie down, holding your crystal comfortably and relax deeply. You might want to prerecord the following on a tape. Visualize yourself walking down a country path, holding your crystal as you go. The sky is blue and the leaves are green. The sun is warm on your skin, but there is a gentle breeze that cools you. You can hear the birds singing and smell the scent of blossom, new-mown grass and the all-pervading aroma of the earth. Beneath your feet the path is springy and even. Be aware that life is like this path. Your life is like a path. What sort of path is your life? Is the path you are walking along changing to represent your life? How is it different? Is it rocky, meandering or overgrown? Or is it straight and clear? Continue with your walk for a while.

YOU WILL NEED

Jasmine oil; an oil burner; your crystal, preferably in a ball or egg-shape.

4 Now notice that dusk is beginning to fall and there is a slight mist rising. Ahead is a bend in the path. You go round this and you find yourself at a crossroads. You are not sure which way to go, so you hold your crystal a little tighter. Ask it to show you which way to go.

5 Down one of the paths you see a faint glow. You realize that this is emanating from a much larger version of your crystal, totally filling the path ahead. Walk down the path towards this. What do you see on the path and around you? Are you meeting people, seeing animals, plants, buildings? Or hearing music? Or smelling, tasting or touching anything? As you draw close to your crystal you see how beautiful and wonderful it is. Slowly approach it until you are close. Try to look through it at what lies beyond. Is there a door forming in the crystal? If so, pass through and continue your journey.

6 When you are ready, come back properly to everyday awareness by patting yourself all over. Write down all you have seen. You may just have seen hints and symbols, or you may have had a revelation about the next step to take in life. Cleanse your crystal and repeat as necessary.

YOUR PROTECTION CRYSTAL

—

Most crystals have protective qualities because their calming and balancing influence has a beneficial effect on the environment. However, your Protection Crystal is intended to do more than that and can strengthen your inner and outer defences by adding its energy to yours.

Occultists and clairvoyants tell us that we all have an aura – a sheath of energy surrounding the body that appears in many different colours and layers. A clairvoyant may be able to discern characteristics such as strength and spirituality in the aura. Although you may not realize it, a strong and vibrant aura can offer you protection against many things, because it is sensed at a subconscious level by those who might cause harm, and also because it repels negative energies generally while attracting positive ones. With its sympathetic vibrations your Protection Crystal can help to strengthen your aura.

Often the most obvious threats are the easiest to deal with, while the subtle ones may be more insidious. For instance, it can be difficult to identify and confront a person who is leeching your energy or undermining you. Your Protection Crystal can deal with the problem where it starts – at the energy level. However, it is important that you also take practical action to keep yourself safe. For instance, while garnet protects against attack, your best defence is to keep away from dangerous neighbourhoods. One of the most valuable gifts offered by your Protection Crystal is that it strengthens your intuitions about safety.

CHOOSING YOUR PROTECTION CRYSTAL

The following crystals have been selected for their variety of protective qualities, but each one can have the effect of strengthening your own protective abilities and instincts in all areas.

YOU WILL NEED

Choose from malachite, labradorite, bloodstone, snowflake obsidian, garnet, chalcedony, lapis lazuli, jet, onyx, jade, carnelian and red jasper. Dark-coloured ribbon, candle; lavender oil and joss stick.

THE CLOTH BAG METHOD

Simply place the crystals or their substitutes in a cloth bag. Close your eyes, become calm and state clearly from what you want to be protected. Ask for guidance, reach into the bag and take your pick.

THE VISUALIZATION METHOD

This method is an expansion of the above, but will give you the opportunity to tune in to the spirits of the crystals. You may like to prepare for it with a cleansing bath in which you have sprinkled a little essential oil of lavender. Play relaxing music to get you in the mood and burn a pleasant joss stick.

Make sure you won't be disturbed. For this method it is truly necessary to have each of the crystals, at least in the form of tumble-stones, set out before you. Prepare for the exercise in the same way as the circle method, but before imagining your fear, visualize a spirit rising out of each crystal. If your powers of visualization are good, you may see them forming quite clearly and you may feel you can communicate with them. One may seem especially powerful and sympathetic and you may feel drawn to this one. If you do not feel clear, visualize your fear as described below. Now observe which of the crystal-spirits goes forth to do battle with and destroy your fear.

THE CIRCLE METHOD

Arrange the ribbon in a circle on the floor with the crystals (or representations) in a line, roughly towards the north of your circle (or south if you live in the southern hemisphere). Light a candle to stand behind the crystals and place yourself inside your circle of safety. Take with you something that makes you feel safe, such as a picture of a friend, or even a teddy bear you loved as a child.

Affirm that you are safe, close your eyes and become calm and steady. Visualize your fear materializing behind the candle. Even if it is something formless, like depression, give it a shape if you can, or failing that a sound, smell or sensation. Now ask yourself which crystal is going to zap that fear. Visualize a white laser-beam striking the fear and destroying it. The crystal that produces the white beam is your Protection Crystal.

IF YOUR CHOICE DOES NOT FIT

Maybe you were worried about your child, yet your choice has been carnelian; or your career concerns you, yet jet has come forward. Trust your crystal – while it may seem as if you are doing the choosing, the truth may be the reverse. So use the crystal that has 'picked' you, adapting to suit; place carnelian near your child's bed as well as your own, place jet on your desk as well as over your hearth. Improvise and combine until you feel sure where the true need lies.

INTERPRETING YOUR PROTECTION CRYSTAL

BLOODSTONE

Since ancient Babylonian times, bloodstone has been credited with the ability to repel enemies. Soldiers carried it to prevent wounds and halt bleeding, and even today it may be used to stop nosebleeds, no doubt simply through the coolness and pressure of the stone. If this is your choice then you may fear literal cuts, threats to your physical vigour, or you may have to undergo an operation.

Bloodstone keeps anything harmful at bay and strengthens your own ability to avoid danger by using your wits and common sense. Wearing bloodstone protects your health. Hold it below the waist, for strength.

Bloodstone keeps you CONNECTED to the here and now, so that you can be FOCUSED and EFFECTIVE.

CARNELIAN

This is a wonderful stone for courage, protecting generally from negativity and the harmful influences of the past. It is especially good for public speaking, something that is increasingly required professionally and of which many people are afraid.

Carnelian was also believed to guard against others knowing your thoughts or against 'enchantments'.

Carnelian guards the home against storms, keeps anger and spite at bay, and it drives away the fear of death. If you have chosen this stone then you are aware that you need a major dose of strength, confidence and vitality, but also to feel peacefully aligned to the cycles of life.

Wear carnelian as a pendant for a continual source of ENCOURAGEMENT and to advertise the fact that you are a FORCE to be RECKONED with.

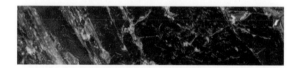

GARNET

This is a very strong stone, bringing with it powers of endurance and great energy. If you have chosen this stone, you may be facing a particular challenge, either physical or mental. Garnet will protect and conserve your energy levels. In times gone by it was thought to drive away demons and to warn the wearer of approaching danger.

Garnet will strengthen your auric sheath and if you visualize this, your 'vibes' may discourage a would-be attacker. Traditionally garnet offers protection against thieves and it is also beneficial for health. If you feel 'there is no way out' garnet will help you find one and turn you into a survivor. Wear as earrings to sense any approaching threat.

Wear garnet as CLOSE to your HEART as you can to feel EMPOWERED.

CHALCEDONY

This stone protects against bad dreams and negative thinking. It also dispels illusions of all kinds and alleviates sadness. If you have 'the jitters' it can calm you and may also be effective for more extreme types of mental disturbance. It has long been considered a protective talisman for travellers, preventing accidents and mishaps, and it protects the home and the family.

If you have chosen this stone, you may be deceived by a person or situation – or deceiving yourself. At an instinctive level you realize this and have come to chalcedony to dispel this. Or it may be that you are moving around a lot and face instability – chalcedony can bring you encouragement, faith in yourself and feelings of joie de vivre. This stone also offers protection in lawsuits.

Wear chalcedony as a RING or necklace to feel cared for and SAFE in the WORLD.

JADE

Jade has many protective qualities. It is especially good for protecting the body from disease, and will also protect your plants if four pieces are placed around the edges of your garden, roughly at the compass points. Because it brings wisdom it averts bad judgement and stops you being manipulated. In the same way it prevents accidents.

The Chinese believe that jade prolongs life and eat from jade bowls to absorb the benefits of the stone. If you have chosen jade, you may sense your best protection is to tune in to the benefits of Nature, to seek peace, care for your body and go with the flow. Jade heals the kidneys and bladder and may be worn on the belt, or anywhere next to the skin for maximum effect.

Jade brings HARMONY and ATTRACTS FRIENDS.

RED JASPER

Jasper works on many levels to keep you safe. It protects you from your own desires, which could lead to danger. In ancient times jasper was believed to protect against poisoning and to guard mother and child during childbirth. It repels all negativity, sending it back to the source. If you have chosen this stone, you may feel you need to get a handle on things, face conflict if you have to and be honest with yourself.

Jasper helps to keep you grounded and to nurture yourself in tough times. Best of all, it helps you put your finger on what is wrong before it gets out of proportion, and it enables justice to be done. Place it close to the base of your spine to feel detoxified or wear as jewellery.

Red jasper is a stone of HEALTH, strength and VITALITY, increasing BEAUTY and attractiveness.

JET

Jet is not really a crystal, but fossilized wood. It has been used for protection since the Stone Age. Placed on a newborn baby's stomach it guards the child. Worn as an amulet it protects the traveller in strange countries. Jet is also a protection when embarking on inner journeys such as visualizations, and it guards the health.

If you have chosen jet, you may possess deep knowledge from many incarnations, and realize that your best protection is experience and the wisdom of the planet Earth. Jet is a very receptive stone and is believed to merge with the body of the owner, so pre-owned jet should be cleansed assiduously. Wear jet as a necklace to take control.

Jet REPELS nightmares and all SPIRITS of EVIL and DARKNESS.

LABRADORITE

This stone of psychic protection will strengthen the aura and preserve its energies. It will guard you particularly from the thoughts of other people, especially their unconscious expectations and beliefs about you. Labradorite will make it impossible for these to attach to you and subvert you. If you have chosen labradorite, you may recognize that your main purpose is a spiritual one and you wish to hold to this and avoid contamination.

Labradorite will also help you resist base impulses and distractions. It repels all negativity, including your own as you become aware of it. It can be worn as a necklace over the heart or held for inspiration and to balance the bodily processes.

Labradorite stone will be a SUPPORTIVE COMPANION through CHANGE.

LAPIS LAZULI

In ancient Sumer this stone was closely associated with deities, so wearing it invoked the protection of the gods. It is also associated with the great Egyptian goddess Isis. It protects the bond between lovers. In modern day India it is used to protect children who wear it as a necklace to keep them healthy and to help them grow.

If you have chosen lapis lazuli you may be especially aware of the need for loving, caring and nurturing thoughts, both from yourself and those around you, to protect the interests of those you love. It enables you to remain calm and able to say the right thing at the right time to promote your best interests. It is best worn at the throat.

This stone REPELS SUFFERING and CRUELTY.

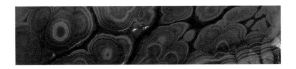

MALACHITE

This stone is believed to warn the owner of impending danger. According to legend, malachite will break in pieces as a sign that danger is approaching. It protects financial affairs, especially if placed at the four corners of an office or building. A very powerful stone, malachite needs to be used with care as it magnifies all energies, including negative energies. It absorbs pollution.

Mostly, however, malachite protects from stagnation, so if you have chosen it you want to preserve your ability to transform and move on, even if this might be uncomfortable at times. Use only polished malachite. Place it on your navel to recover from old traumas or wear as preferred.

NOTE: Remove malachite at once if you experience palpitations.

Generally, malachite GUARDS against NEGATIVITY and physical DANGER, especially danger from falling.

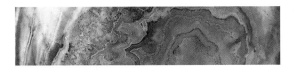

ONYX

Onyx protects against enemies of all kinds; it can help to reduce the sexual urge so offers protection against rape or being carried away by your own passions if they are misguided. If onyx is your choice you may feel vulnerable and want to keep your head down and shut off generally. Possibly you are afraid of exposing yourself or letting yourself down.

This stone will keep your secrets. Onyx will give you stamina and the strength to look beyond present challenging circumstances into a more promising future. Wear onyx on your left hand (if right-handed) to harmonize with the restrained character of the stone.

Onyx is GROUNDING and SUPPORTING, a stone to lean on and to learn from when gaining CONTROL of your life.

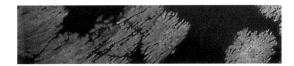

SNOWFLAKE OBSIDIAN

All forms of obsidian are highly protective for they block and mop up negative energy. Snowflake obsidian is a gentler form of the stone, and is less likely to demand self-analysis from you. If you have chosen this stone, you may be afraid of fear itself, frightened by your own negative thinking. Or you may be truly under attack on a spiritual level from someone who is sending ill wishes your way; only by fearing this can you let it through your defences.

Snowflake obsidian will strengthen your faith in yourself and enable you to feel solidly in contact with Mother Earth. Hold snowflake obsidian against you, very low down on your abdomen, to give you 'guts' and imagine it forming a dark, protective cloak around you.

This stone is PROTECTIVE and is able to ABSORB NEGATIVE energy.

PROTECTING YOUR CHILD RITUAL

Several stones are good for protecting children: lapis lazuli and malachite from the list on page 90 and also amber and agate. However, if a stone has 'spoken' to you as your protective influence, then this is the stone that will best amplify your protective intention to make it strong and durable and effective.

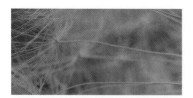  

1 Do this ritual when your child is asleep so that you will be able to concentrate. Place the crystal under her or his bed and, if you have an oil burner, heat patchouli oil for its protective and grounding influence. Light four white candles to symbolize the earthy balance of the four directions. (If you fear the candles may wake your child, this ritual can be performed without them.)

2 Visualize an egg of light emerging from the crystal. See it expanding and glowing until it locks into the aura of your child. Imagine this protective egg around your child. No harm can possibly penetrate this egg. See your child smiling and happy, enjoying life within this egg. Affirm that the 'egg' will allow love and communication to pass its membrane while keeping all harm at bay. Hold and elaborate for as long as you like.

3 When you feel ready, remove the crystal and extinguish the candles and oil burner. The crystal can now be passed over the child's clothes, pushchair and belongings for added protection. Cleanse the crystal and repeat when you wish. It may be best not to leave 'strong' crystals such as malachite in your child's room.

YOU WILL NEED

Patchouli oil; four white candles.

CRYSTAL SPIRIT DEFENCE VISUALIZATION

If you are coping with a threatening situation or person at home or at work, this visualization will boost your ability to look after yourself and ensure that you have a powerful ally on the subtle planes brought by your crystal.

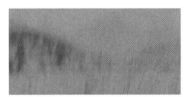

1 This is an expansion of the visualization method for choosing your crystal (see page 90), and may be prepared for in a similar way, by bathing and playing music. A patchouli joss stick is a good choice, but lavender, frankincense, pine and rose are also linked with protection and will help you to 'tune in'.

2 Place your crystal in front of you surrounded by four candles set in a protective square to symbolize the four directions. A large piece of crystal – a pyramid, wand, cluster or ball – would be good here. Relax and watch the reflections of the candles in the crystal.

3 Now visualize an angel rising out of the crystal. See it take shape, growing to life size, becoming brighter and more detailed. Try to see your angel's face; speak with it if you can. Ask your angel to be with you and protect you. See that your angel has a sword or other weapon that shatters deceit and repels all spite, attack and negativity. This weapon is effective against negativity – it does no harm to anyone although anyone malevolent will be repelled. Ask your angel to stand behind or beside you and to remain with you. It will stay with you, but may gradually fade, so boost its strength by drawing on your crystal again, with this exercise, as necessary.

SELF PROTECTION RITUAL

This exercise strengthens your auric sheath, so that you will be safe from harm. It draws on the powers of the Earth and your own special crystal, to create 'generators' to boost your aura. Try to obtain two or more pieces of your crystal – one to wear, one for work, one for home and so on. Wearing your crystal is good all-round protection, but having a large crystal where you can see it is a great additional boost.

1 Many of us feel threatened and this can be a barrier to progress and happiness; this exercise is of great benefit so set aside a few peaceful hours to give it your full attention. Go for a walk in the country or parkland and find a sizeable flat stone, perhaps 12 cm (5 in) square – take your time with this. Cleanse this in a stream or soak later in spring water for an hour.

2 Have a relaxing bath containing a few drops of lavender oil. Arrange your area with the lit candle in the south symbolizing fire, the stone in the north (for earth), the joss stick in the east (for air) and the wine glass in the west (for water). These are associations that have been used by occultists for centuries. If you live in the southern hemisphere, reverse earth and fire, since the sun is in your north. Place your string or ribbon in a circle around your body.

3 Start by facing your stone and say 'May the powers of earth enter this crystal, protecting from all physical harm.' Imagine physical strength and barriers, affirming that your crystal holds this. Now turn to the east saying 'May the powers of air enter this crystal, protecting from mental harm and harsh words.' Imagine bright, pure thought and an ability to 'rise above' entering your crystal. Face the candle and say 'May the powers of fire enter this crystal, giving spiritual protection, courage and energy.' Imagine your crystal vibrant with inner fire. Face the wine glass saying 'May the powers of water enter this crystal, protecting the heart and emotions, and healing.' Imagine your crystal holds soothing waters or amniotic fluid as in the womb.

YOU WILL NEED

A joss stick of patchouli, lavender, pine, frankincense or rose; a wine glass filled with spring water; an orange or gold candle; 6 metres (20 ft) of string or ribbon in a dark colour that means safety to you. You may take a teddy bear (or similar) with you.

4 Turn back to the stone and place your crystal/s on it. Visualize an energy-beam coming from this now formidable crystal, strengthening your aura until it is intense, strong and impermeable.

5 To finish, extinguish the candle, pour the water from the glass out on to the earth and bind the string around the stone. Keep this safe, to use again. Affirm that you are back in the here and now by patting your body all over. Store your crystals as appropriate. Whenever you need an extra burst of protective power, look at your crystal and imagine that energy-beam coming towards you again. You are protected on all sides and in all ways.

YOUR
MEDITATION
CRYSTAL

—

Meditation is an altered state of consciousness in which your mind has access to inspiration and insight, or a means to experience a oneness with the world that is very healing and uplifting.

There is nothing strange about this state of mind, since we approach it whenever we daydream, although we may fail to realize its power. Meditation also includes visualization and inner journeys. All such practices are helpful in today's hectic and materialistic environment.

The crystal you choose for meditation will enable you to leave this world behind and to enter a peaceful alternative reality that some call the astral plane. Occultists believe that on this plane the imagination is very powerful, and that things you wish to create first take shape there, before being translated to ordinary reality. Your crystal can help you focus your true wishes clearly and effectively, by aiding your ability to visualize.

However, please do not worry if you find it hard to visualize, for it is possible to gain the benefits of meditation in peace and stillness.

CHOOSING YOUR MEDITATION CRYSTAL

Choosing your meditation crystal is a 'meditation' in itself. Find a quiet place where you won't be disturbed and set aside time to determine which of the following crystals will aid your meditation practice.

YOU WILL NEED

Choose from amethyst, ametrine, clear quartz, black obsidian, chrysocolla, golden beryl, celestite, sodalite, rhodochrosite, green agate, selenite and azurite. Purple or violet candle.

THE VISUALIZATION METHOD

Make certain that you will not be disturbed while you meditate. Burn a purple or violet candle and place your tumble-stones, or their representations, around it. Sit or lie down comfortably. Relax and become aware of your breathing. In your mind, go to a place in the real, natural world that you love and with which you have a special affinity – this may be a woodland clearing, a lakeside spot, a rocky beach or whatever comes to your mind. Take as long as you like to imagine this.

Be aware of an entrance to a cave in your peaceful place. Go towards it. Deep within the cave is a light, similar to that of your candle, only much brighter. Around it are grouped the spirits of the crystals in a shimmering cluster, radiant with divine blessings.

Ask the spirit of your crystal to come to you, to guide you. Wait patiently. The spirit that comes to take your hand is your guide on inner journeys. You may now journey further with your crystal spirit or give thanks and come back to everyday awareness.

Make a note of your experiences in your notebook. If this visualization does not work the first time you try it, repeat the method until it does.

THE CHAKRAS

The chakras are important to meditation. These are organs or centres in the spiritual body – the body that has its existence in the astral plane but which occupies the same space as your physical body. Some people are able to leave their physical body and travel consciously in the astral plane, while we all do this nightly in our dreams. Deep meditative states have some elements in common with astral travel.

As you meditate it is likely that your chakras – essentially energy centres – will be activated. Certain crystals have an affinity with specific chakras. There are seven main chakras to consider. These are situated on the crown, the brow, the throat, the chest, the solar plexus, the lower abdomen and the base of the spine.

Starting with the base chakra and the colour red, they correspond, in order, with the seven colours of the rainbow. Crystals are often linked to a chakra because of colour correspondence. Full instruction on opening the chakras is outside the scope of this book, but when you use your crystal you may be aware of one or all of your chakras opening. It is very important that you close them after each exercise, or you could feel depleted and open to unpleasant influences, either from disturbing humans or spirit entities. Do this by imagining them shutting tightly like flower petals reverting to bud and by affirming strongly that you are closing down, and/or by eating and drinking.

The Base Chakra relates to survival and the organs of elimination (and sexuality to some extent). The Sacral Chakra relates to the sexual organs and is about intimacy and deep feelings. The Solar Plexus Chakra relates to the central nervous system and digestion, also to the sense of self, development and creativity.

The Heart Chakra is naturally related to the heart as an organ and to all it connects with, and spiritually to the capacity to love, empathize and feel compassion. The Throat Chakra is concerned with the speech centres and the ability to communicate. The Brow Chakra is the 'Third Eye', relating to the brain and more subtle perceptions. Finally, the Crown Chakra is our link with the Divine and with true enlightenment.

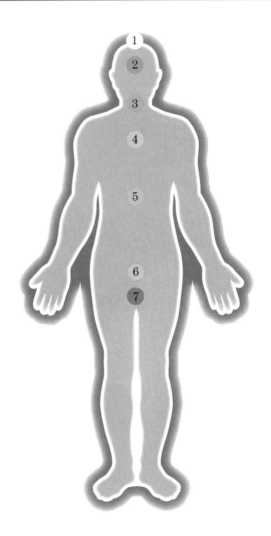

1–Crown Chakra, 2–Third Eye Chakra, 3–Throat Chakra, 4–Heart Chakra, 5–Solar Plexus Chakra, 6–Sacral Chakra, 7–Base Chakra.

INTERPRETING YOUR MEDITATION CRYSTAL

AMETHYST

This wonderful purple stone is extremely spiritual and protective. If you have chosen this stone, you may already be attuned to higher states of consciousness, or have a deep desire to be so. Amethyst links with the Third Eye Chakra, and if you place it on this part of your body it can open your perceptions. It connects you, gently and completely, to the realms of spirit and the inspirations of the astral plane.

Meditating with amethyst facilitates astral travel and sleeping with it under your pillow will bring revealing, yet peaceful dreams. Your choice of amethyst shows deep understanding, a profound tranquillity but also the sense of adventure to explore the subtle realms.

This stone confers wisdom, but also acts as a GUARDIAN against INVASION on the spiritual planes, TRANSMUTING negativity into love.

AMETRINE

This crystal is a combination of amethyst and citrine, formed as heat within the Earth was transforming amethyst into citrine. It brings with it the spiritual gifts of amethyst along with the mental clarity of citrine. If you have chosen this stone, you may want to be able to make intellectual sense of your insights and to be able to use them creatively in the earthly realm.

Place ametrine on your solar plexus to coax deep issues to the surface, enabling you to express them clearly, so freeing yourself to explore and create without excess baggage. Meditating with ametrine enables you to embrace paradox and unite the masculine and feminine sides of your nature.

Your choice of ametrine shows DYNAMISM and a wish to control your own life, drawing on WELLSPRINGS of wisdom and UNIVERSAL love.

GOLDEN BERYL

This is called the stone of the seer and was the original 'crystal ball'. The crystal of the Elizabethan occultist Dr John Dee, now housed in the British Museum, is made of beryl. It is a wonderful stone for scrying (see scrying rituals on page 108). It is associated with the Crown and Solar Plexus Chakras. If you have chosen beryl, you may long for a less stressful life where you can leave behind the tedious and unimportant and concentrate on spirituality and fundamental priorities.

Placed on the solar plexus, beryl enables you to relax completely; placed on the top of the head, it encourages total focus and may bring strong insights. Choosing beryl indicates that you want to sort out your priorities and manifest what is really important in your life.

Beryl allows you to start sorting out your priorities. This starts with effective and very clear use of the IMAGINATION to CREATE on the ASTRAL plane.

AZURITE

This stone facilitates astral travel and may help in channelling. This is a process where an individual may deliver messages from the subtle realms. If you decide that you have the ability to channel, you will find you are saying things almost without the intervention of your conscious mind. Your choice of azurite indicates that you wish to communicate on a higher level, although this may not take the form of literal channelling, but may mean you want to convey your spirituality to others.

Azurite helps you let go of old, outworn beliefs, especially fears and phobias, which it helps you to understand and transmute. Help for this may be received during meditation, with azurite on the throat or Third Eye (see page 103).

Choosing azurite shows that you SEEK a NEW REALITY.

GREEN AGATE

Agate has a strong connection to the natural world and the Earth. If you have chosen green agate, you may be powerfully aware of the divine in Nature and are able to enter mystical states through contact with plants and trees, or you may sense that you could develop this.

If you meditate with green agate on your Heart Chakra, it can open you to a profound love and compassion for all that lives on the Earth, and in turn you will feel nourished. This stone stabilizes and balances. If you have been emotionally traumatized it will enable you to see the bigger picture, to be soothed and to move on in life.

If you have chosen green agate you are DECISIVE (or would like to be) and able to find PRACTICAL SOLUTIONS to problems.

CHRYSOCOLLA

This tranquil stone enables you to find and maintain inner peace when all around you is in a state of flux. If you have chosen this stone, you may wish to stay in contact with the spiritual essence within you to help you cope with insecurity and instability. Or you may be blessed with the knowledge that change brings opportunity and you are able to go with the flow.

Chrysocolla may be placed at the Heart Chakra to heal sorrow and enable love to flow anew. At the Throat Chakra it facilitates calm, clear communication and confers the wisdom to know when silence would be best. If you have been feeling burdened by guilt, meditating with chrysocolla on your heart will enable you to forgive yourself.

Choosing chrysocolla SHOWS STABILITY and SERENITY.

CLEAR QUARTZ

This crystal holds the key to the widest possible range of knowledge and wisdom. If you have chosen clear quartz you are a seeker after truth and may want the answer to fundamental questions. Quartz can increase your energy, both physical and spiritual, and may be placed on any of the chakras for corresponding benefit. It also has the gift of harmonizing the chakras, regulating the energy flow in your subtle body, making you alert, yet tranquil and very clear in mind, emotions and spirit.

Clear quartz can release buried memories, both from this life and former lives, and helps you to develop your psychic abilities and awareness.

If you have chosen clear quartz you have psychic energy that you wish to focus, but you need to be FREE of DISTRACTIONS and achieve BALANCE.

CELESTITE

This New Age stone is similar to angelite. Avoid leaving it in sunlight or its delicate colour will fade. Celestite is a great boost towards spiritual development. If you have chosen this stone, you may feel that you want a push to enable you to begin exploring new forms of spirituality. Celestite will lead you to fortunate contacts that will help you on your path. It facilitates dream recall and astral travel, but it also brings peace and strength.

Celestite is especially helpful when placed on the Third Eye Chakra where it tunes you in to Universal wisdom. Choice of celestite may mean that you need to leave mundane worries behind. It helps you to combine your intuition with your intellect to feel sure of your path and to communicate this clearly and peacefully.

Celestite placed anywhere in the room will RAISE vibrations and is GOOD for GROUP meditation.

SELENITE

This stone has a very fine vibration. If placed in water it dissolves, so do not cleanse it this way. It brings incomparable peace and is said to facilitate contact with angels. If you have chosen selenite, you may have deep within you a concern for your past lives and evolutionary path, and instinctively wish to be on the right track. This stone enables you to check, intuitively, whether you are fulfilling the tasks necessary in this lifetime.

You may also be aware of angelic messengers and wish to encourage them. Selenite resonates with the Crown Chakra and is deeply spiritual, so if you have chosen it you may wish to develop this side of yourself.

Selenite also helps TELEPATHIC CONTACT, especially if each person involved HOLDS a piece of selenite.

BLACK OBSIDIAN

This is an extremely powerful stone. There is no messing around with black obsidian; it will haul the truth up out of the depths so that it can be confronted and transmuted. Use this stone with care and be sure it is right for you. If you have chosen black obsidian, you may feel you need to face certain aspects of yourself and/or certain memories before you can progress spiritually.

Black obsidian will help you transform, changing negative to positive. It will also confer strength and protection. Placed on the Solar Plexus Chakra, this stone brings subtle energies into the body and has a grounding effect. Scrying with obsidian may result in prophecy, but this should be used with care.

Your choice of obsidian shows COURAGE, and a WISH to MOVE forward.

SODALITE

Sodalite induces deep meditative states, fostering the search for truth and idealistic values. If you have chosen sodalite, you seek the conviction to stand up for your beliefs, coming from a position not of believing but knowing. Sodalite sweeps away dogmatism and blinkered thinking, enabling both intuitive understanding and objectivity.

Placed on the Third Eye Chakra, it enables you to have a true understanding of your situation in life. Sodalite increases self-esteem and self-reliance, so that you can practise what you preach. It also helps you to accept the things about yourself that are shadowy and unpleasant, without judgement or guilt.

This stone indicates that you want to be FREE of preconception and indoctrination, to find your own CONNECTION with the DIVINE.

RHODOCHROSITE

This warm pink or orange stone encourages you to open your Heart Chakra to trust and to love. If you have chosen rhodochrosite, you may want to access inspiration from your subconscious in order to be artistically and creatively inspired. You may have been hurt or abused, and you realize that only by getting to the root of this and releasing it can you switch on to the Universal love that is all around. You can facilitate this by placing rhodochrosite on the Solar Plexus or Base Chakras while relaxing.

Rhodochrosite helps you to accept all your feelings as natural. Choice of this stone may indicate that your emotions have been a barrier to meditation, or that you have an ardent desire to be an active, loving and spiritual participant in the world.

This is a very positive stone and can also help to achieve SPIRITUAL EXPERIENCES through SEX and perceive its SACREDNESS.

SCRYING MEDITATION

Scrying is actually crystal gazing, although you can scry using almost anything with a reflective surface, even a bowl of water. As you look deeply into your speculum (the object you are using for scrying), you are tuning into images in your subconscious that may be helpful, revealing or even prophetic. Your own meditation crystal is the perfect vehicle for you to look within and beyond.

1 Scrying is a solemn matter and it is better to do it when you feel strong and upbeat; if you are depressed you may call negative images your way or interpret things badly. Prepare for scrying by first taking a bath or shower, possibly using lavender soap for spiritual cleansing. Affirm that you are clear, calm and protected – it is a good idea to visualize a protective circle of light around you.

2 It is best to scry in a darkened room. If you light a candle it helps to set the scene, and you may prefer to scry with the candle flame reflecting in the surface of your crystal. Moonlight is even better. In an oil burner, heat oil with an uplifting fragrance such as frankincense or sandalwood.

3 Sit in a relaxed way with your crystal in your lap or on a flat surface in front of you – the larger your crystal is the easier you will find this, and the clichéd crystal ball is best of all. However, it is possible to scry with a small, rough stone. If your stone is very small, then place it beside a bowl of water and use the water as your speculum.

YOU WILL NEED

Candle, frankincense or sandalwood oil.

4 If you have a question, ask it clearly in your mind before you start. Allow yourself to become dreamy, almost as if you are about to go to sleep, but without feeling tired. Look deeply into your speculum, as if you were looking into another world. Soon you should see images – some people experience these as if they were literally 'seeing' them, others see with the 'mind's eye'. You may not see anything, but you may find that you hear, feel, taste or even smell things. Your crystal can put you in touch with messages in many different ways.

5 Make a note of all you apprehend and anything that goes through your mind in your crystal notebook. Even if something does not appear to make sense, it may become apparent later. Sometimes things you see can be alarming, but a skull, for instance, can mean ancestral wisdom, so you should always look for a positive interpretation.

6 When you have finished scrying, imagine a clear, sparkling stream running through your crystal, cleansing it of any impurities. Wrap it up in black velvet and put it away safely. Make sure you have come back fully to everyday awareness by patting your body and affirming that your protective circle has vanished. Stamp your feet to reconnect with the earth and take a drink of water or tea. If you practise scrying regularly, your talents will develop.

REACHING OUT TO YOUR CRYSTAL ANGEL VISUALIZATION

This visualization will help you make contact with the spirit of love and wisdom to which your crystal is a portal. It is intended to be a deeper and more intimate encounter than you made when choosing your crystal. Here your crystal spirit is not only companion and guardian but teacher.

1 Prepare for this exercise in the same way as for scrying, by bathing and heating oil in an oil burner, as this helps to get you in the right frame of mind. Settle yourself where you can relax totally. Place your crystal in front of you where you can see it as you enter your inner world. You may prefer to record the following instructions on tape before starting the ritual.

2 Imagine that it is the cool of evening and the bright crescent of the new moon hangs in a lilac sky. You find yourself at the foot of a beautiful mountain, made solely of the substance of your crystal. You touch the sides to find that they are smooth and invite caress. Now notice a staircase cut into the side of the mountain. You begin to ascend the steps slowly and smoothly.

3 Higher and higher you climb and as you do so, the shadowy landscape stretches around you and beneath you. Up and up you go, where the air is pure and clear, until you come to a platform where the staircase ends. There is a door with a silver handle leading into the mountain. Gently turn the handle and walk in.

4 You find yourself in a place of breathtaking beauty. The walls within the crystal mountain sparkle and shimmer. The chamber extends far into the distance and the ceiling is high. A subtle light illumines everything. There is a sound of soft music and a scent of incense. You feel full of wonder.

5 At the far end of the chamber the light seems to be growing. You watch as it increases in intensity and you realize that a being of great power and beauty is coming towards you. This is the angel of your crystal. He or she will appear to you in the way that is best to communicate with you.

6 Greet your angel in any way that seems appropriate. Ask her or him any questions that you have and listen carefully to the answers. Your angel may say things to you unbidden, and you should listen to these as well. Your angel will have a gift for you; this may be something abstract, like love or courage, or something real and symbolic, such as a book. Whatever this is, treasure it and give thanks. Pledge also a gift of your own that seems appropriate, such as a loving act. Remain with your angel as long as feels right.

7 When you are ready, take leave respectfully, make your way to the door and down the mountainside. When you reach the bottom, come back to everyday awareness. Pat yourself to make sure that you are back in the here and now, and have a drink of water or tea. Record all that you have experienced in your notebook.

8 Each time you travel to meet your crystal angel you will be forging a stronger connection with the spirit of your crystal. This will help to foster peace, wisdom and a deep knowledge.

ENHANCING YOUR LIFE WITH CRYSTALS

—

Crystals can be used to enhance your life in many ways. Constructing a mandala has powerful psychological benefits, while using crystals in the home can increase your sense of well-being. They can also be used to stimulate dreams and to ease you through the various rites of passage that are part of our human experience of life.

H aving taken the trouble to select your eight personal crystals, you will want to involve them in your life. As always, the most important guide is your intuition. If it feels right to place a crystal in a particular spot in your home, to arrange them in a certain way or to carry them with you, then that is fine.

Remember also that things change as time goes by, so what works for you and seems right at one point may subsequently alter. If you do decide to make changes, it is best to introduce these singly, and gradually, so you can see how they work.

The crystals themselves may 'teach' you to make changes, and that includes the way you use them! Crystals sometimes 'want' to be given away, for instance, and this could mean that the person to whom you give them has, for now, a greater need and affinity. If you feel this leaves a gap in your life, rest assured that it will be filled.

In this final chapter you will find several exercises for using all your crystals together to expand your consciousness. Follow these, or experiment for yourself, and enjoy your crystals.

YOUR CRYSTAL MANDALA

A mandala is a circular pattern, which is a symbol of wholeness. The analytical psychologist Carl Jung discovered that the mandala is a powerful symbol in the growth of self-awareness because it signifies the entirety of the human psyche in perfect balance. A person who is complete has their emotions, physical sensations, thoughts and spirituality in harmony. Of course this is a very difficult state to achieve, but on an instinctual level the sight of the mandala is an inspiration towards this state.

When you lay out your crystals in this circular, mandala formation you are sending a strong message to your subconscious that you are in harmony internally and with the world around you. Setting out a mandala shape is a small ritual that brings peace.

To arrange your mandala at its best you will need all your crystals to be a similar size. If you were to have one very large, another as a wand, another as a ball or pyramid and the remainder as tumble-stones, the appearance of the mandala would not be as satisfying. You will need also a stone or large pebble that you have picked up on a walk, and found especially attractive. This is placed at the centre of your mandala. Alternatively, you could use a pair of Boji stones, since these are very grounding. However, these are not easy to obtain. Another good stone for the centre is staurolite or

Fairy Cross. These are twinned crystals that form a cross and so symbolize the four elements of air, fire, earth and water in balance.

Magic practitioners traditionally perform rituals within a magic circle – another mandala shape. Around the circle, four quarters are marked and associated with their elements: north with earth; east with air; south with fire; and west with water. In the southern hemisphere exchange the positions of earth and fire, since the sun (naturally linked to fire) is in the north sky. These elemental links are relevant when you lay out your Crystal Mandala, because some crystal meanings are more readily linked to certain elements. However, remember that all these instructions are just suggestions; if some other pattern or association appeals to you, then feel free to follow it, since that is what holds meaning for you.

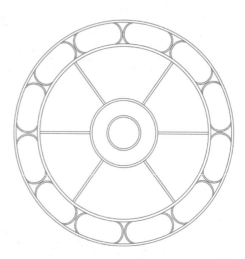

LAYING OUT YOUR CRYSTAL MANDALA

When laying out your mandala for the first time, make sure that you feel relaxed and harmonious. Play soft music, light a candle, burn a joss stick or lavender oil in a burner. Choose a place where you feel happy. You may like to set aside a shelf or cupboard-top on which to leave your mandala permanently. If you do this, remember to cleanse your stones from time to time.

---

1 Start by placing your stone, Boji stones or staurolite in the centre of what will be your mandala. Locate the approximate position of north and place your Protection Crystal here since earth is linked to protection and grounding (use south in the southern hemisphere). Opposite, in the south, put your Success Crystal, because success links to your own personal 'sun' shining brightly (north in the southern hemisphere). In the east, the direction of sunrise, place your Personality Crystal since air is linked to self-expression. In the west, home of healing water, place your Healing Crystal.

2 Now place your Money Crystal in the northeast (southeast in the southern hemisphere), as it partakes of solid cash (earth) and abstract figures (air). Put your Love Crystal in the southeast (northeast in the southern hemisphere), where it has the heat of fire and the mobility of air. Place your Relaxation Crystal in the southwest (northwest in the southern hemisphere), moving towards the peace of water but retaining the playfulness of fire. Put your Meditation Crystal in the northwest (southwest in the southern hemisphere) linking the healing energies of water and the protection of earth. Meditation is a very inward and mystical pursuit, and north is a very special direction, magically, because it is the dark and mysterious quarter of the sky (reverse in the southern hemisphere). Many magical practitioners place their altar in the north of the circle (south in the southern hemisphere). However, all this is suggestion, your own feelings are paramount.

3 As you lay out your mandala, work clockwise in the northern hemisphere, anti-clockwise in the southern hemisphere, because in this way you are moving in the same direction as the sun and moon are seen to move in the sky, harmonizing with Nature.

4 When your mandala is complete you may like to reaffirm the elemental associations by placing a candle by your Success Crystal, a joss stick by your Personality Crystal, a wine glass of water near your Healing Crystal and a bowl of soil near your Protection Crystal.

5 Your mandala is a thing of beauty and a personal affirmation of your inner harmony and development. Lay it out whenever you feel the need to rebalance yourself or go inwards. Gaze at it, reflect awhile and experience peace.

DIVINATION USING YOUR CRYSTAL MANDALA

Your Crystal Mandala is very personal to you, and so it is a key to the wisdom of your unconscious. If you are uncertain which path to take in life or have an important question to which you need the answer, you can use your mandala for guidance.

YOU WILL NEED

Night-light candle, jasmine oil, herbal tea containing cinnamon; paper.

THE SCRYING METHOD

You can use your mandala to help you to scry. Scrying was explained in the previous chapter, but you can refine it in this way. Set out your Crystal Mandala, but instead of your Meditation Crystal, set a lighted night-light candle in its place in the circle. Then place your Meditation Crystal in the centre of the circle. Hopefully, you will have a larger version of your Meditation Crystal for scrying purposes.

Move the smaller crystals and the night-light up close to your Meditation Crystal so that they are almost touching (not so close that the crystals become hot, however). Burn some jasmine oil in your burner. Herbal tea containing cinnamon – another 'psychic' herb – may also stimulate your awareness. Relax, ask your question and begin gazing.

THE PAPER METHOD

Another way to use your mandala for divination is as follows: write your question or problem on a small piece of paper. Set out your mandala and hold the piece of paper about a metre (a yard) above it. Let the piece of paper go and see which stone it falls nearest to. This stone has the answer to your question. If it is close to two or more stones then you may remove the other stones and repeat, or you could place the stones in question in a black bag and draw one out. This is the stone with the answer.

If the paper falls so far outside the circle that you feel unsure which one to choose, repeat the process. If you repeat it three times and still do not get anywhere near any answer, then you should leave the matter and try again after a few days.

Your intuition will lead you towards an answer once you know which stone is relevant, or you could meditate by relaxing as explained in the chapter 'Your Meditation Crystal' while holding the crystal that has the clue. See what comes into your mind.

While it is possible that a fully-fledged solution will appear in your mind, it is more likely that you will be guided in a direction that will prove helpful. Some suggested interpretations begin as follows:

- **Protection Crystal** You need to look after yourself, ground and nurture yourself, concentrate on your welfare and those you love.
- **Money Crystal** The answer concerns your funds, earning power, material possessions and their value.
- **Personality Crystal** Your self-expression and self-development are the issue – be yourself.
- **Love Crystal** The issue concerns your partnership or romantic concerns. Possibly love is coming into your life. Be loving.
- **Success Crystal** This is about career matters, your future, your life path – this is lucky.
- **Relaxation Crystal** You need to unwind more, the issue concerns your spare time and how you use it.
- **Healing Crystal** You have a need to heal yourself or others. Look after yourself; be gentle with yourself.
- **Meditation Crystal** Now is the time to go inwards, retreat, commune with yourself, seek privacy.

While we naturally want guidance and a glimpse of the future, the purpose of divination is to bring us closer to the 'divine', however you define it. If you are anxious about the future this exercise will probably bring you greater peace, even if the answer is unclear.

MANDALA MEDITATION

If change is an issue for you, this exercise performed with your Crystal Mandala can ease things. If there is heavy loss involved, such as bereavement, the presence of trusted friends and family can help.

1 Heat cypress oil in your burner to ease grief. Lay out your Crystal Mandala and in the centre place a symbol of the loss you feel. This may be a photo if the loss concerns a loved one or pet. If it is the end of a relationship it may be a ring. If you have moved house but still miss your old home then a picture of the old house could be included. If it is a job that you have lost then anything that links you to it, such as letterhead paper, might do.

2 Place the black and white candles and your symbol into your mandala. Look at your symbol and reflect on the past. This has ended and is making way for something new. Say 'I bid farewell to all that has gone before. In love and peace I let go. In love and peace I move on.' You may say more if you wish.

3 When you are ready, snuff out the black candle and move the white candle and the symbol out of your mandala. If you are saying goodbye to a loved one, you might like to move the memento or photograph to a special shelf where you can make a temporary shrine, placing the white candle beside it along with examples of your Protection Crystal, Meditation Crystal and, most especially, your Healing Crystal. These should be crystals specially acquired for the purpose, not the ones from your mandala. Also place here a sprig of rosemary, which signifies remembrance. However, please do not enshrine old relationships or jobs because they need to slip away into the past and have no hold on your heart. Symbols of such matters need to be burnt or buried, and the white candle extinguished after this. Burn them in a heat-proof container, such as a saucepan and say a thorough goodbye.

YOU WILL NEED

Cypress oil, orange oil; three candles (black, white, orange).

4 When you have disposed of your memento, light a big orange candle in the centre of your mandala and place cheering orange oil in your burner. Say 'New things await me, life is full of hope and promise.' Look at the flame and imagine new, good things coming your way. You can repeat this ritual if you need to.

5 If you are recovering from something really bad, such as an abusive relationship, then please do not place any reminders within your mandala. Place any such items outside your mandala, flanked by two black candles. Say 'I banish all .... from my life. I reject it utterly. I am protected from it. I destroy all links and move away.' Burn the memento with determination and a great sense of release and snuff out both candles. When this is complete, light the orange candle inside your mandala, burn orange oil and say 'I am free, I am cleansed, I am strong, I am new. I go forward into a new future.'

CRYSTAL RITES OF PASSAGE

Nothing in life is certain except change and yet change, especially when it involves loss, can be very difficult to cope with. However, the peace and completeness of your Crystal Mandala can help you to have faith in the Universe and in your own ability to adjust and move on. Your Crystal Mandala is very personal to you, and so it is a key to the wisdom of your unconscious. If you are uncertain which path to take in life or have an important question to which you need the answer, you can use your mandala for guidance.

There are many passages in life. Some are personal, others are part of the experience of all humanity. These include menarche/adolescence, marriage/committed relationship, giving birth, menopause and bereavement. Other changes that may be quite stressful are moving house, losing a job, starting a new job, ending a relationship or starting a course of study. Only you can decide how difficult you are finding the particular change you are undergoing. Each person has their own individual reaction, and while some people find even quite large changes stimulating and exciting, for others a minor shift may cause intense anxiety. If you are not quite sure how you feel, reflect for a while holding your Meditation Crystal and try to be honest with yourself.

MENOPAUSE RITUAL

Menopause should be a time of new beginnings and opportunities, although in our culture this does not always seem so because older women may not be valued.

ADAPTING THE RITUAL FOR MENARCHE

For menarche, light the red candle from the white and snuff out the white. Say 'I move into the bloom of my Womanhood. I can carry life within me. May I be blessed' and proceed as above. For a young girl who has not acquired her Crystal Mandala, a simple gift of garnet, ruby or other red stone is a lovely way to mark the transition.

1 Adapt the exercise on page 118, using red and white candles (black is too sombre) or any colour/s of your choice. Snuff out the red candle and leave your white or favourite coloured candle in your mandala while you light your orange one. Say 'I move away from my motherhood into my role as wisewoman. I laugh, I create, I enjoy life, I am free!'

2 Have a treat such as your favourite wine or chocolate. If possible, obtain your Success, Personality, Love or Relaxation Crystals (your choice) as beautiful jewellery. Place this within your mandala and put it on after lighting the orange candle.

PARENTHOOD RITUAL

If you have recently given birth or become a father try this simple ritual to welcome your child into the world.

1 Place a picture or symbol of your child within your mandala, with two lit white candles and a third pink candle. Also place a small rose quartz heart near the symbol. Light the pink candle from one of the white candles and say 'I embrace my new role as a mother/father. May love guide me, may my mind be clear and my heart true.' Take up the rose quartz and hold it while affirming your intentions.

2 Let the white candles burn down by a picture of your child. Place the rose quartz heart with your child's things. Keep the pink candle to reaffirm your love from time to time, just by lighting it and reflecting. This exercise can be adapted for the start of any loving relationship. A ring or other jewellery could take the place of the heart. Words could be 'I devote myself to this new relationship. May love unite us and our hearts be true.'

YOUR CRYSTALS IN THE HOME

Crystals make beautiful ornaments and can be used to enhance any décor. Choose them to complement your colour scheme – the crystals and the room will be enhanced and brightened; colour is a vibration and crystals will strengthen its beneficial effects. Crystals also make wonderful gifts for they have personalities of their own and can never be duplicated even if you already own a similar crystal.

Certain crystals obviously have a natural home in specific rooms. For instance, you may want to place your Protection Crystal near your doorway, your Relaxation Crystal in a sitting room or bedroom, Money and Success Crystals on your desk and so on. It is always best to go with what you feel is right. However, it is a good idea to bear in mind the Chinese system of Feng Shui when placing crystals.

Feng Shui means 'wind, water' and refers to the subtle powers of the natural world on particular spaces. The space we live in is a metaphor for our lives and how we use specific parts of our space has an effect on the fortune that we experience. Feng Shui is a complex system, but there are some very simple things that can be done. The rule is to make only small changes, to wait while they take effect and not to meddle too much where things are fine. Thus, if your relationship is going well, there is no need to place a crystal in your Relationship Corner, because that could make things just too hot to handle. But if you need more money, then the Money Corner is a really good place for your Money Crystal.

MAPPING YOUR HOUSE

The usual Feng Shui map goes like this. Taking your bearings from your front door, immediately on your left is the area connected with knowledge. Going clockwise, at a right angle to you on your left is the family area. The far left corner of the house relates to money, the area far in front of you relates to fame and to the right of that is the relationships area. Still moving clockwise, at a right angle on your right lies the area concerned with children/creative works, and immediately on your right is the friends/helpful people area. Your entrance itself relates to your career and the very centre of the house or flat is Tai Chi or balance.

Naturally your chosen Money Crystal may find a home in the Money Corner, your Success Crystal in the Fame Corner and your Love Crystal in the Relationships Corner. For the other crystals, you may move them about as appropriate. An area of life that needed protection, healing or more relaxation could have any one of those crystals positioned in it. It is better not to make too many changes at once – just place one crystal in the important spot and wait a month or two to see what happens.

Individual rooms may be divided just like the house, so if you have one room that is very much yours, for instance because it is your study or bedroom, it can be taken to have its own Money Corner, Relationships Corner, and so on; you can place crystals accordingly. Crystals have beauty and power. Let them enhance your home.

STIMULATE YOUR DREAMS

Dreams are the language of your unconscious and if you listen to them, they can tell you many things about yourself and your life. You may also find that your dreams tell you about the future and give you answers to questions.

We all dream every night, but not everyone can remember their dreams and some people assert that they don't dream. They are mistaken; all it takes is a little encouragement and your unconscious mind will reveal a magical territory for you to explore.

1 Start by placing your crystal notebook by your bed along with your Meditation Crystal. You could place your crystal under your pillow. Tell yourself that you are going to dream, that you will remember what you have dreamt and take notice. In all probability you will wake the next morning with some recollection of a dream. However partial and trivial this may seem, write it down, for in this way you are delivering a strong message to your unconscious that it is being listened to. Be prepared to jot down dreams in the middle of the night, if that is the only time you are aware of them.

2 When you feel reasonably confident of your ability to dream, prepare for a 'dreamy' night by having a bedtime bath and drinking a soothing herbal tea such as camomile. Traditionally, jasmine has been used to induce prophetic dreams, so some jasmine flowers under your pillow or a dab of jasmine oil will help. So much the better if you are able to do this at the full moon.

3 When you are ready for bed, choose one of your crystals to be your companion. This may be any crystal, not just your Meditation Crystal, since you are going to use the crystal as the start of a dream-journey. Pick the one you most want to get lost in at the present moment. There may be an issue that is bothering you: for instance, if you have relationship worries you may want to journey within your Love Crystal and ask a specific question. Or it may be that you are more drawn to one crystal at the present time.

4 Settle yourself on your bed ready for sleep and gaze deeply into your crystal in a way similar to that used for scrying. Formulate a question if you have one. Let the crystal surround you and imagine that you are going inside it – it is enormous, surrounding you, you are within it. You may see all sorts of things or you may see only the crystal. Focus your eyes on the distance and keep looking. Other bodily sensations may come to you and you can take note of them but don't let them divert you. Continue looking within the crystal, staring, striving to look beyond, deeper, until your eyes become tired. Place the crystal beside the bed and try to keep looking at it while you are falling asleep.

5 In all probability you will have a memorable dream that night. In fact, you may have one that is very vivid. The dream may contain an answer to your question or it may be ambiguous. Take note of all you see – some of it may be symbolic but the meaning will come to you if you give it time. Be very sure to write everything down in your notebook.

INDEX

ACKNOWLEDGEMENTS

PICTURE ACKNOWLEDGEMENTS

123RF akispalette 63al; akispalette 84; Daria Minaeva 73, 96; Dmytro Denysov 74al; Gennadiy Poznyakov 72b; lukaszs 79; olivierl 39b; serezniy 19; Sophiejames 109; V S Anandha Krishna 26. **Dreamstime.com** Alexey Poprotskiy 43; Assistantua 21al; Jiri Vaclavek 44bl; Milosz Aniol 77ar, 85c; Nongnuch Leelaphasuk 113br, 121l; Pavel Shykuts 21r; Penchan Pumila 32al; Shshphotography 113al. **Octopus Publishing Group** (crystal photography) 1-128. **Pixabay** 24b, 31, 63ar, 89br, 96al. **Unsplash** Adrian González Simón 101bl; Ales Krivec 64, 72al, 75r, 102; Alex Klopcic 10, 17bl, 24al; Alex Ruban 61b; Anna 41br; Anna Jimenez Calaf 74b; Anthony Delanoix 61al; Ashley Batz 29bl, 38c, 74ac; Bady Qb 117; Ben White 39ac, 41cl; Benjamin Child 28, 38l; Chris Ensey 37; Clem Onojeghuo 17ar; Colin Maynard 29ar, 38r, 75l; Conrad Ziebland 61ac, 62ac, 88, 97l; Daniil Kuzelev 65al; David Boozer 119; Dawid Zawila 53 bl, 62ar; Dean Hayton 112; Deniz Altindas 113cl; Denys Nevozhai 17cl, 25r; Ellen Jantsch 24ac; Emma Hall 52, 60al; Erol Ahmed 29br, 36c; Felipe Elioenay 11, 53cl, 62al; Freestocks 49b, 65cl, 72ac; Gabriel Santiago 24ar, 53al, 60ar; Gaetano Cessati 89bl, 96ac; Galen Crout 17al, 25c; Guillaume de Germain 65bl, 72ar, 73ac; Hans Vivek 53br, 60ac; Igor Ovsyannykov 65ar, 75c; James Mcgill 61ar, 101cl; Jan Kahanek 13; Jay Castor 6r, 17br, 62b; Jez Timms 53ar; Jon Phillips 29al, 36l, 74ar, 99; Jose Murillo 51, 113; Josefa Holland Merten 100; Kari Shea 65br, 73al; Katherine Hanlon 29cl, 36r, 67; Larm Rmah 101ar; Linda Xu 6l, 76, 84al, 85ar; Lukasz Szmigiel 2, 27; Matt Antonioli 87; Meiying Ng 40, 49r; Melissa Askew 39al, 41ar, 63b; Michael D Beckwith 113ar, 121r; Mike Enerio 50; Mr Robot 15, 89al, 97c; Neil Thomas 39ar, 41al; Nick Karvounis 89cl, 96ar; Peter Hershey 77cl, 84ac; Priscilla Du Preez 7 101al; Ray Hennessy 77bl, 84ar; Ren Ran 77br, 89ar, 97r; Ruben Engel 77al, 85l; Sebastian Unrau 101br; Steven Kamenar 6c, 41bl, 49al, 91; Sven Owsianowski 55; Todd Quackenbush 16, 25l; Yoann Boyer 60b.